ROMAN

EST

D

er

nal Studies
er
14

Westall

Cover: Roman fort at Housesteads

ISSN 0308-4310

ISBN 0-901-272-09-4

This volume is the fourteenth in a series of occasional papers in which contributions to the study of the North West are published by the Centre for North-West Regional Studies in the University of Lancaster and are available from there. The general editor will be pleased to consider manuscripts of between 10,000 and 25,000 words on topics in the natural or social sciences and humanities which relate to the counties of Lancashire or Cumbria.

PREVIOUS TITLES

Windermere in the Nineteenth Century
Working Class Barrow and Lancaster 1890 to 1930
Handloom Weavers' Cottages in Central Lancashire
Flowering Plants and Ferns of Cumbria
Early Lancaster Friends
Traditional Houses of the Fylde
Peter Newby: 18th-Century Recusant Poet
North-West Theses and Dissertations 1950–1978: A Bibliography
Lancaster: The Evolution of its Townscape to 1800
Richard Marsden and the Preston Chartists, 1837–1848
The Grand Theatre, Lancaster: Two Centuries of Entertainment
Popular Leisure and the Music Hall in Nineteenth-Century Bolton
The Industrial Archaeology of the Lune Valley

Printed by Mather Bros (Printers) Ltd Preston

CONTENTS

		Page
Preface		v
Acknowledgements		vii
List of Selected Dates		ix
1. Introduction		1
2. Conquest		5
3. Consolidation, A.D. 83–120		20
4. The Northern Frontier		30
5. Roman and Native in North-West England		41
6. The Last Years		63
7. Conclusions		72
Appendix	I—The Brigantes, Venutius and Cartimandua	74
	II—Known Dispositions of Roman Units	75
	III—Dated Building-work at North-West Forts	77
Notes and Abbreviations		78
Bibliography		79

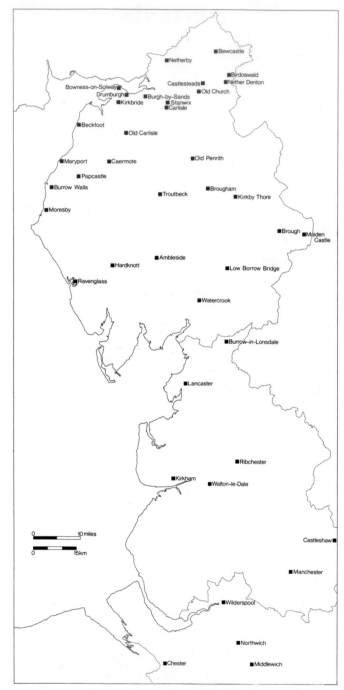

Fig. 1   Roman North-West England

PREFACE

The Romans are always with us. Of course, this is the case in a deep cultural sense. But it is equally true topographically. It is easy to see how the situation and layout of such cities as Carlisle, Lancaster and Chester are a product of their Roman origins. It is almost certainly equally true of many smaller towns and villages, though the evidence has either been destroyed by later development or has not yet been unearthed.

Dr Shotter points out that increasing resources allowed archaeology to boom in the 1970s. Public interest in the value of sites encouraged official and private bodies to countenance 'rescue' digs in advance of development projects. These changes allowed many important new sites to be excavated and assessed. Energetic departments of archaeology at Lancaster and Manchester Universities and the commitment of local county councils to archaeological work have ensured that the North West has seen its fair share of these developments. This is important, for there had been a tendency for the region to be seen in terms of the course of the original invasion and in its role as a route to the northern frontier, rather than in its own right.

Dr Shotter's own research has made him an authority on the Roman period in the North West. Furthermore, many enthusiasts have found his earlier popular work the foundation of their understanding of the subject. His extensive experience with local archaeological societies has given him a special insight into the interests of amateur archaeologists and the difficulties they encounter in appreciating professional work. In this book he draws together the considerable research carried out in the last fifteen years, to provide a new picture of the region in the Roman period. He shows how the indigenous tribal society adapted considerably to colonial rule; that an integrated economy and society evolved which was sufficiently attractive to its members and contained an adequate stability to wish to prolong itself after Roman military power had for all practical purposes evaporated. However, he points at all times to the gaps in the evidence and the problems of its interpretation, so that the reader is given a real flavour of the difficulties faced by the archaeologists attempting to deepen still further our understanding of the Roman North West.

Oliver M. Westall

ACKNOWLEDGEMENTS

Although the views expressed in this book are ultimately my own, the preparation of it would have been impossible without the assistance of a number of people: Philip Howard, Experimental Officer in Archaeology at Lancaster University, produced the maps and plans, whilst Joe Thompson of the University's Media Services Unit did a great deal of work on preparing the photographic material. Dr Timothy Potter, now of the British Museum, not only gave general encouragement in his inimitable way, but also permitted the use of a number of his own photographs. Mrs Janet Atkins and Miss Rosemary Hoggarth between them shared the task of preparing the typescript. Last, but not least, Marion McClintock lent her own style of encouragement at various stages, without which all might have faltered at an earlier hurdle.

David Shotter

List of Selected Dates

A.D.

43 Roman Invasion of Britain from South East (Northern England—Brigantia—'tied up' by the establishment of a political arrangement with its queen, Cartimandua).

60–69 Likely Roman intervention in the southern Pennines as the political arrangement broke down.

69 Civil War in Rome: northern England becomes openly hostile.

71–72 Roman troops invade Brigantia under Cerealis—crossing the Pennines at Stainmore and probably reaching Carlisle.

79 Full invasion under Agricola; route established from Chester to Carlisle; 'termination' established by the Stanegate from Corbridge to Carlisle and westwards to Kirkbride.

80–84 Agricola in Scotland; withdrawal to Forth/Clyde line in or soon after 84.

84–120 Consolidation of North West England; new forts established in Lake District (Watercrook, Ambleside, Hardknott, Ravenglass, Old Carlisle, Caermote, Papcastle, Maryport); industrial site at Wilderspool (Cheshire) established to supply the garrisons; older (Agricolan) forts rebuilt.

c. 100 Withdrawal from southern Scotland; strengthening of Stanegate, first with a signalling system, then with forts.

110–120 Disturbance in the north.

120 Building of Hadrian's Wall and associated coastal system as far south as Maryport (?).

143–163 Occupation of Antonine Wall in Scotland: temporary abandonment of Hadrian's Wall.

c. 163–215 Continued disturbance in the north until peace secured with the Picts by the campaigns of Septimius Severus and subsequent 'diplomatic initiative' of his son, Caracalla.

c. 230 Some form of civilian administration established around the Carvetii (a sub-group of the Brigantes) based upon the developing town of Carlisle.

250–300 Apparent decay of some forts, perhaps indicating presence of caretaker garrisons—or even abandonment. This was followed by rebuilding on the northern frontier late in the third or early fourth centuries under Constantius, the father of Constantine.

c. 330 New, bastioned forts being built on the west coast (like Saxon shore forts in the east) at Cardiff, Caer Gybi (Holyhead) and Lancaster.

367 'Conspiracy of the Barbarians'—attacks on all fronts, followed by large-scale rebuilding under Count Theodosius, with especial attention being given (apparently) to the coasts.

c. 400 Last supplies of coins reaching Britain—so presumably few soldiers left to pay.

410 'Formal' severance of control by the emperor, Honorius.

1
Introduction

The physical environment of North-West England presents marked contrasts, which will have played a large part in determining the patterns of conquest and occupation by the Romans. The mountains of the Lake District are bounded on three sides by coastal plain, and on the fourth by the communications corridor represented by the Eden and Lune rivers. Initial Roman strategy took account of the difficulty of this terrain by arranging its domination through control of the Eden and Lune valleys.

Further south, a broad contrast obtains between the Pennine foothills in the east and the coastal plain in the west. This coastal plain is itself penetrated by the valleys and broad estuaries of the Mersey, Ribble, Wyre, Lune and Kent rivers, which flow from and forge connections with the foothills. Conquests here consisted of control of the valleys and their interconnection by means of a north/south control of the foothills.

Equally obviously, the environment dominated the nature of settlement—in ways that ranged from the broad shape of the rural economy to matters such as the availability of building-stone and other raw materials. Clearly there were factors which presented different conditions from those obtaining today—the changing nature of the coastline, afforestation, climate—but current evidence suggests that in general exploitation of the landscape was on an impressive scale. Research in the Lune, Eden and Kent valleys has indicated the deliberate positioning of farms to employ both the arable soils of the valley floors and the grazing potential of the valley sides; nor should we lose sight of the fact that pollen analysis has pointed to the growing of cereals to a greater altitude than is currently the case. Similarly, the positioning of farms on the lower slopes of the Lake District hills enabled both arable and pastoral potential to be exploited.

Further, if deforestation was a phenomenon of the later Roman period, this will point to an added enhancement to the 'produce' of the rural economy in the shape of red deer and swine. Beyond this, however, this deforestation reflects not only the considerable Roman demand for timber (for building and heating), but also the need for land for agricultural usage. In its turn, this fact may suggest not so much that the Roman presence acted as a magnet, but that the Roman occupation itself thrived because of the economic vibrancy of the area. In this way, as experiments are demonstrating dramatically in southern Britain, the environment provided the means of support for the Roman garrisons of occupation.

From this it comes as no surprise that North-West England contains a wealth of archaeological sites of all periods, from the prehistoric to the modern. The Roman period is no exception: legionary fortresses, auxiliary forts, fortlets, watch-towers and temporary marching-camps provide the evidence of the military occupation by the Romans, whilst civilian life is attested in small towns (*vici*), industrial sites, farmsteads and at least one major urban centre (Carlisle). Connecting such sites is a network of roads, some of whose routes can still be easily traced on the ground.

However, whilst this abundance of sites has long been appreciated—except, perhaps, those of an agricultural nature—work on understanding them properly has been relatively slow, since until the 1960s most excavations were small in size. Although small-scale trenching *can* produce dramatic and inspired results, there is no doubt that the provision of financial resources in recent years on what, by north-west standards, has been a lavish scale, has enabled work to progress faster and more systematically. In the last decade, we have seen large-scale excavations at Chester, Northwich, Manchester, Wilderspool, Ribchester, Walton-le-Dale, Lancaster, Watercrook, Old Penrith and Carlisle, as well as at Burgh-by-Sands, Bowness-on-Solway, Biglands House Farm, Cross Hill Farm (Penrith), Troutbeck, Brougham and Maiden Castle-on-Stainmore—not to mention highly significant sites like Vindolanda and Housesteads which, although on the outer boundaries of the geographical scope of this book, have produced results with important implications for the understanding of north-western sites. As well as this, funds (both public and private) have been provided for aerial reconnaissance which has not only told us much about known sites, but also (particularly in the rural context) shown up large quantities of sites whose existence was not previously suspected.

At the same time, a good deal of work has been done on the recorded finds from north-western sites—the inscriptions, pottery and coins and coin-hoards—which has enabled our understanding of the history of the Roman occupation to be refined considerably. Yet it is as well to remember that still only a tiny percentage of the area covered by Roman sites has been sampled, and that we are therefore still in great danger of producing interpretations and hypotheses which future work will show to have been untenable.

Inevitably, since it is threatened sites which attract funding, excavation has to take place not necessarily where we believe that problems will be solved, but where rescue threats exist. Recent excavations at Watercrook demonstrate the risks this may cause: that work was concerned principally with the civilian settlement (*vicus*), for that was where the rescue work threat existed. However, we now know enough to realise that it can be dangerous to hypothesise about the chronology of a Roman fort on the basis of evidence which derives from its *vicus*. In other words, until a major internal fort building is stripped, our views on the fort itself remain largely in the field of conjecture.

Thus, although we can assert with confidence that knowledge has advanced considerably in recent years, there are still many fundamental gaps in that knowledge. Most north-western forts still lack a detailed chronology, and some even a basic chronology. There are major sites whose nature is still in doubt, such as Walton-le-Dale and Kirkham. There are areas where we may guess that sites existed, but where so far little has been found; for example, Furness and Fylde—in particular whether there may have been major sites at places such as Barrow and Fleetwood; there is also the vexed question of a possible site at Wigan. Again, the place-name of only one Roman site (Bremetennacum/Ribchester) can be asserted for certain, and this shortcoming leaves us in almost total ignorance of the changing garrison-pattern at north-western forts. We are accumulating knowledge about rural

2

settlement, but it is certain that a large number of relatively ephemeral earth-work sites must have perished in the face of the plough, and with them substantial numbers of temporary marching camps for the army on campaign. Such earth-work sites tend to survive well only on marginal land, not subject to plough damage. As to the towns, so important a feature of Romanised life, Carlisle has yet to yield a plan of a single complete building, whilst the smaller towns (*vici*), are known only in fragments, and pose considerable problems in chronological interpretation.

Until we progress further on such questions, ignorance will continue to surround the most important question of all—how did Roman and native coalesce into a Romanised social and economic unity, assuming of course that they did? Thus, whilst this book will attempt as coherent a view as possible of the Roman North-West, many of the views expressed here are necessarily hedged around with caution. Hopefully, therefore, this book is at one and the same time a report and a challenge.

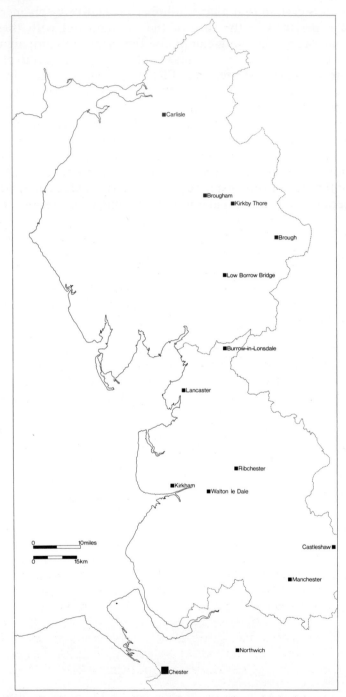

Fig. 2   Roman military sites occupied at least as early as Agricola's governorship

4

2
Conquest

The Roman invasion of Britain began in A.D. 43; by the early 50s, the tribes of southern England, the Midlands and South Wales had been defeated and formed into the new province of *Britannia*. Beyond lay territory more intransigent; North Wales was at once the home of Druidism and a haven for refugees from further south, such as the spirited leader, Caratacus. Northern England, with the exception of a strip on the east coast of Yorkshire, was populated by the tribe known to the Romans as the Brigantes; they are described by the Roman historian, Tacitus, writing at the turn of the first and second centuries A.D., as the most populous of all the British tribes. Their territory stretched northwards into southern Scotland, to judge from the discovery in Dumfriesshire of a relief-carving of the Romanised tutelary deity, *Brigantia*. Culturally, it is likely that the Brigantes, whilst probably ruled by intrusive leaders with affinities further south, were a Bronze Age people, made up of arable farmers, pastoralists, horse-breeders and metal-workers.

Our information about the Brigantes in the period leading up to the full Roman intervention in the 70s comes mainly from three passages in three different works of Tacitus.[1] Tacitus had some knowledge of Britain, which he had gained from his father-in-law, Julius Agricola, who was governor of the province between A.D. 78 and 84. Whilst, however, Tacitus' *Agricola* – the biography of his father-in-law—describes the province and its people in some detail, the *Histories* and *Annals* provide an account of Roman history in the first century A.D., and British affairs form only a small portion of them. Further, as is usual with Tacitus' accounts of provincial affairs, the British passages are not without difficulties in interpreting both chronology and topography.

It would appear—and the point seems to take confirmation from the number of hillforts amongst the Brigantes—that whilst the tribe may have owed a titular allegiance to a paramount monarch, local control fell to a number of smaller hegemonies. The chief contenders for leadership amongst the Brigantes were Cartimandua and Venutius, the latter said by Tacitus to be second only to the great Caratacus as a warlord. Venutius was anti-Roman, whilst Cartimandua courted Roman support for her position by entering into an alliance with Rome—an alliance which evidently made Venutius see that he was better served by appearing to support than to oppose her. Cartimandua showed her good faith to Rome by handing over Caratacus to the Romans, whilst they in their turn returned the compliment in A.D. 69 by rescuing her when Venutius eventually managed to oust her from power.

Where their respective seats of power were located is hard to say, though the archaeologist, Sir Ian Richmond, suggested that Cartimandua's ability to rule the tribe stemmed from the fact that she controlled the richly fertile land of the Vale of York, perhaps even having her centre at Eboracum (York)[2]. Venutius' centre is harder to fix, though Roman military activity in the 60s in the southern Pennines might suggest strength there; further it seems more than coincidence that the

Stanwick fortifications in North Yorkshire were being vastly enlarged at the same time that Venutius was taking control of the tribe and preparing to face Rome.

It is evident from Tacitus that the relationship between Cartimandua and Venutius was a tense one, and that it in no way softened Venutius' anti-Roman stance. Roman intervention in Brigantia was evidently necessary under at least two early governors— A. Didius Gallus (A.D. 52–57) and Vettius Bolanus (A.D. 69–71), although we should note the contrasting views on Bolanus of Tacitus who regards him as inactive, and the late first-century Roman poet, Statius, who implies fierce action during Bolanus' governorship.[3] Further, although this intervention persuaded Venutius to bide his time, it was certainly not easy action for Roman troops. However, patient as Venutius had been, the opportunity created by the Roman Civil War in A.D. 68–69 was too good to miss, and it was then that he ousted Cartimandua and turned a neutral kingdom into a hostile neighbour requiring urgent Roman attention.

The bulk of activity concerned with the Roman conquest of the Brigantes dates to the Flavian period (that is, during the reigns of Vespasian and his sons Titus and Domitian—A.D. 69–96). As we have seen, however, the difficult relationship between Rome and the Brigantian leaders necessitated some earlier activity. However, the location of this pre-Flavian action has long been a matter of speculation, although it is usually assumed that the forts at Templeborough (near Rotherham) and Chesterfield[4] date from the 60s, as do forts which separated the Brigantes from the Parisi, their neighbours on the Yorkshire coast. How far north this pre-Flavian action extended west of the Pennines is hard to say, though there is some evidence from finds (though not, as yet, structures) that Walton-le-Dale (near Preston) may have seen Roman troops in the 60s. In any case, however, this in no sense amounted to conquest in the region; this was left to two Flavian governors in particular— Q. Petilius Cerialis (A.D. 71–74) and Cn. Julius Agricola (A.D. 77 or 78–83 or 84).[5]

However, the allocation of activity to the two governors is extremely difficult on the basis of archaeological or any other evidence. As Tacitus describes it, Cerialis' activity was largely suited to the immediate needs rather than to a permanent occupation: 'After a series of battles, some not uncostly, Petilius had operated, if not actually triumphed, over the major part of their [i.e. the Brigantes'] territory'. The method, though not precisely described by Tacitus, may perhaps be inferred from an earlier comment about this period[6] when Agricola was commander of Legio XX *Valeria Victrix* during Cerialis' governorship. It appears that the forces were split up, and that therefore in all likelihood Cerialis operated on the eastern side of the Pennines with his old legion, Legio IX *Hispana*, whilst Agricola operated in the west. It is usually assumed that during these operations the fortress of Legio IX was advanced from Lincoln to York, and that Cerialis defeated Venutius at Stanwick, and linked up with Agricola by crossing the Stainmore Pass.

The allocation of sites to this period is, however, hazardous: it may well be, because of their relationship with the road, that the marching-camps across Stainmore such as Rey Cross and Crackenthorpe, date to Cerialis' period.[7] However, the common supposition that he reached as far as Carlisle is as yet supported by no *satisfactory* archaeological evidence. In Lancashire and Cumbria there are as yet no *obviously* pre-Agricolan sites; in any case the difference in artefactual terms between sites of the early and late 70s will be small, although coinage may in some ways be the best guide, since we should expect an early Flavian site to show a more considerable proportion of pre-Flavian coinage. Otherwise, the best guide will be a *stratigraphic* sequence which produces deposits earlier than Agricolan ones. With these two criteria in mind, it is possible that current work at both Ribchester and Walton-le-Dale may offer a possibility of pre-Agricolan activity.[8]

The truth, however, of Tacitus' statement concerning the wide-ranging and bloody nature of Cerialis' activities, and with it by implication their thoroughness and effectiveness, is borne out by two considerations. First, it is evident that Cerialis' successor, Julius Frontinus, was able to operate in North Wales with no fear of being 'stabbed in the back': and secondly, there is the fact that when, after the completion of the Welsh conquest, Agricola turned back to the north, he secured it in a single campaigning season.

Tacitus' account of Agricola's campaign against the Brigantes[9] is unsatisfactory in the extreme if we wish to use it to determine Agricola's precise routes. A number of 'shadowy clues' may, however, be put to work; first, it is evident that the campaign represented a twin advance on both sides of the Pennines—a point which has recently received some corroboration from the discovery in 1974 of a major Agricolan military site at Red House, near Corbridge.[10] Secondly, Tacitus seems to show that Agricola (perhaps reiterating Cerialis' policy) gained the co-operation of the various Brigantian groups by encircling them and thus separating them from their neighbours. This in its turn would suggest a concentration on the chief river-valleys, which effectively separated the defended sites on the high ground. Detail is of course lacking in our knowledge of this, since whilst we can show a considerable number of hill forts, few have been examined with a view to establishing whether or not their dating will tie them into this period. Thirdly, a general indication of topography is contained in Tacitus' remark about estuaries and woods, which applies very well to Lancashire in particular. Fourthly, we may infer from this, and from a remark which Tacitus makes about the joint use of fleet and troops in the later Scottish campaigns, that it was Agricola's policy to disembark troops in the main estuaries and march them up the valleys where they could join with troops taking overland routes. Although speculative in the absence of hard evidence, it might be that the Roman site at Kirkham (whose nature and dating are not certain) started in this way and also for that matter a site which may originally have lain at the mouth of the Wyre, and which many have taken to be Ptolemy's elusive *Portus Setantiorum*.

By stressing Agricola's 'omni-presence', Tacitus has in a sense initiated another area of confusion—namely, he appears to have led scholars to think that every known site in North-West England (whatever its nature) is Agricolan; as Professor Barri Jones wrote some years ago: '"Agricolan" is an overworked adjective'. Fortunately there are ways in which we can distinguish Agricolan from later activity: first, there are some significant differences in the ceramic and numismatic evidence:[11] secondly, by trying to understand Agricola's strategy we can go some way towards working out where we should expect him to have been active. Unfortunately, the most direct form of evidence—that of inscriptions—is largely lacking, because Agricola's permanent forts, built as they were of turf and timber, will have had wooden dedicatory inscriptions, which are likely to have perished. In fact, besides the restored Verulamium Basilica inscription, only one 'inscription' bears Agricola's name—a lead pipe from Chester, dated to A.D. 79.

Of course, a further problem in tracing Agricola's activities is that our evidence, even when we interpret it correctly, derives largely from sites which either became, or were intended to be, permanent. It is possible that other movements of this period remain to be traced through marching-camps. These, because they were occupied only for a short period, leave little occupation-debris for dating, and are in any case likely, as earth-work sites, to be substantially destroyed in an area subject to long-term ploughing. We have seen that there is reason to place the Stainmore sequence of camps earlier than Agricola (although we cannot really call the case *proved*), but we have no real means of dating camps such as Troutbeck[12] and Mastiles Lane (on Malham Moor). It is, however, perhaps worth noting that none of these camps conforms typologically to the distinctive Agricolan camps located in Scotland.[13]

It is a mistake to think, as excavations at a number of military sites have now shown, that a fort of timber buildings, defended by a turf and clay rampart, and entered through timber gateways, is necessarily Agricolan. However, it is the case that Agricola did not leave stone-built forts in his northern campaigns. It is likely that for his campaign in North-West England, Agricola used the near-complete 55-acre legionary fortress at Chester, from where he could advance northwards by land and sea.

The Roman military site at Chester makes sound sense in the context of activity both in North Wales and northern England. It is certain that pre-Flavian material has come from beneath the Flavian fortress which has prompted the suggestion that it may have had a military role as early as Suetonius Paulinus' ill-fated attempt to subdue North Wales. If not then, however, the fortress (as an advance on Wroxeter) must surely have been commenced at the latest by Julius Frontinus in connection with his north Welsh activities in the mid-70s. In this case, we should ascribe its completion to Agricola. Elements of the Flavian fortress have been revealed including well-preserved sections of the turf rampart.[14]

At the same time both Whitchurch and Middlewich have produced evidence of a ceramic or structural nature that is consistent with Flavian activity.[15] Indeed structures seen, though not securely dated, at Whitchurch, may argue for pre-Flavian activity there. On his northward advance Agricola's first fort appears to have lain at Northwich[16] at the intermediate point between Chester and Manchester.

Excavation and observation over the years has established the layout of an auxiliary fort at Manchester on Castlefield (off Deansgate).[17] Recent excavations on the northern and western defences[18] have shown elements of the northern gateway, rampart and ditch-system of a fort which evidently had two turf-and-timber phases, the later of which was approximately an acre larger than the earlier, which was presumably of Agricolan date. It is worth noting that outside the western ditches lay pits interpreted as a defence feature known as *lilia*, into which a sharpened up-turned stake was inserted, and the pit covered with brushwood. A very fine example of this is to be seen to the north of the Antonine Wall, at Rough Castle.

North of Manchester, the situation becomes more complex, even leaving aside the vexed question of Wigan: although a considerable body of circumstantial evidence has long pointed to a Roman site at Wigan—now confirmed by excavation—its nature remains elusive.

The Ribble was certainly a line of penetration and communication; at Ribchester all the evidence points to a foundation at least as early as Agricola, and recent work, particularly in the extended area of the Church graveyard, has given at least a strong hint of earlier deposits.[19] A good deal of the fort's area (approximately 30 per cent) has been lost to river action, but what remains certainly suggests that the earlier period of settlement (that is, the first century A.D.) may have been complicated by reorientation or realignment, perhaps associated with a change in the garrison pattern. Elements of the defences have been observed in a number of recent excavations—a clay and turf rampart rested on a log base (known as a corduroy), and at one point, it could be seen that the turves were approximately one foot square, and that each layer was interleaved with brushwood.

A road ran west from Ribchester on the north bank of the Ribble, making through Preston for Kirkham; as noted above, although finds of Roman material have been made at Kirkham, there is insufficient evidence upon which to base any realistic estimate of the nature or chronology of the site.[20] South of the Ribble, at its

Plate 1   Rochdale: the trans-Pennine route over Blackstone Edge

confluence with the Darwen, lies Walton-le-Dale. Speculation about this site has been intense in the past, but recent excavations appear to have put beyond reasonable doubt the likelihood that the site was military in nature.[21] On the other hand, it has to be said that the buildings so far excavated—and at the time of writing the earliest level has not yet been fully examined—do *not* resemble those of a conventional fort layout. Though of a large scale they would appear to be more consistent with a manufacture, storage and supply role. The possibility, which remains to be fully considered, is that these buildings may be preceded by a conventional fort of Agricolan or even earlier date. If, however, the storage and supply role can be shown to be sufficiently early, then it would also show another element to Agricola's likely use of the fleet to supply his Scottish work.

From both Ribchester and Manchester run trans-Pennine links: from Manchester a road runs across Saddleworth Moor, heading for York; there are forts along it at Slack and Castleshaw. At the latter, there is a large fort, which has timber buildings and which has been assumed to be Agricolan, and a smaller later fort inside it.[22] Another road heads across Blackstone Edge for Ilkley, whilst yet another leads south-eastwards to Melandra[23] and Brough-on-Noe;[24] along this line it is possible that a further Roman site awaits discovery at Whalley—to judge from stray finds of Roman material there. It is likely that the Ribble-Aire corridor was supplied with a

Plate 2   Jeffrey Hill, Longridge: the road from Ribchester to Burrow-in-Lonsdale, which is picked out in the distance by a straight line of hedges and tracks

Plate 3   Lancaster: a section through the Agricolan clay-and-turf rampart

signalling system similar to that identified across Stainmore (see below). Indeed, the existence of a small earthwork on Mellor Hill, above Ribchester, may be a fragment of it; it is further possible that the putative site at Whalley relates to this also.[26]

The military road ran northwards from Ribchester to Burrow-in-Lonsdale:[27] the road itself is still impressively preserved over a number of stretches, although of the fort at Burrow virtually nothing can be seen. The fort, like many, is protected by a confluence of rivers—in this case, the Lune and Leck Beck; it lies at a distance from the main north–south route which prompts the suggestion that it may not be the earliest military site in the area. Limited excavation has taken place, but on the whole tells us more of the later stages of the fort's development than of its initial phases, although it appears that at some stage reorientation occurred. A turf-and-timber phase was located and, although not certainly dated, it would not be inconsistent with an Agricolan beginning.

If that is so, then we can see Burrow as occupying a crucial position in the Lune Valley control system, since it looks in one direction to Low Borrow Bridge in the upper Lune gorge and in the other to Lancaster up to which point at least the river Lune was navigable.

The fort site at Lancaster occupies, rather unusually, a hill-top position. Although it is clear that the sequence of structures, military and civilian, on Castle Hill is complex, we can now be virtually certain of an Agricolan beginning, both on ceramic and numismatic evidence.[28] In the grounds of the old Vicarage, running east–west, was an especially well-preserved turf-and-clay rampart, surviving to a height of

11

1·3 metres. Since this rampart had timber buildings erected across it, we can only assume that later forts were larger, and that the rampart survived because the whole platform had been levelled up. Further, there was no sign of the Trajanic stone rampart to be inferred from *RIB* 604. However, the discovery of a bevelled plinth course on a line that would take it only a few yards north of the clay and turf rampart suggests that on the north side at least the enlargement was not great. If this was the northern defence of the Agricolan fort, it is likely that the western defence of the same fort was located in western Vicarage Field in 1971.[29] On the other hand, although an eastern gateway was found near the junction of Church Street and China Street, there was no evidence there of a turf-and-timber phase, suggesting that the eastern rampart of the Agricolan fort must have been higher up Castle Hill. It is also

Plate 4   Caton: Roman milestone of Hadrianic date (now in Lancaster City Museum)

12

Plate 5   Tebay: the road to the south of Low Borrow Bridge

worth noting that at some stage before it went out of use, this turf rampart underwent a modification, possibly indicating a short break in occupation in the later Flavian period—a suggestion which would not be at variance with the numismatic record.[30]

A road running on the south bank of the Lune towards Burrow is certainly attested in the Hadrianic period (*RIB* 2272), joining the Ribchester–Burrow road possibly at its crossing of the Wenning.[31] The upper Lune was protected by the fort at Low Borrow Bridge (Tebay), the outline of which is still clearly preserved. Excavation of the site has been limited,[32] and the dating evidence, although consistent with pre-Hadrianic activity does not require a date as early as Agricolan. However, it does not seem reasonable that Agricola did not establish a site in this area: thus either an Agricolan site awaits location or, rather like Lancaster, and as suggested by Hildyard,[33] the Agricolan fort was a smaller one situated within the area of the later fort.

At Brougham, the north–south route joined with that coming across Stainmore. As has already been noted, it has always been held that since the Stainmore road is clearly earlier than the marching-camps (Rey Cross at least), then the road belongs to the period of Cerialis, the structures to Agricola—a probable, though not inescapable, conclusion.

Four marching-camps are known in the area—Rey Cross and Crackenthorpe, Kirkby Thore and Plumpton Head. These camps were intended for legions on the march and are therefore simply defended areas in which tents could be pitched. The finest of them is undeniably Rey Cross with its near-complete circuit and entrances

Plate 6 Rey Cross-on-Stainmore: the Marching-camp. The figure on the right is inside the camp; that in the centre is on the rampart; and that on the left is on the *tutulus*-mound

defended by outer covering mounds (*tutuli*). The shapes of these camps are by no means as regular as those of the permanent forts: indeed, whilst Rey Cross is nearly square, Plumpton Head forms an irregular trapezoidal shape.

In addition, a line of permanent forts crosses the pass—from Greta Bridge through Bowes, Brough and Kirkby Thore to Brougham. Between Bowes and Brough is the much smaller fort of Maiden Castle. Of these, Greta Bridge and Brougham have usually been assumed as Agricolan foundations, although there is no proof: at Kirkby Thore[35] a turf-and-clay rampart inside the later fort may be Agricolan, and a similar defensive arrangement was attributed to Agricola at Bowes.[36] Brough-under-Stainmore has seen some excavation,[37] though in the case of this fort, it is the chance finds of coins and pottery that point to an Agricolan foundation rather than anything structural revealed by the excavations themselves. Finally, the fortlet at Maiden Castle, which covers approximately half an acre, may well have been more concerned with a signalling and watching role than employed as a garrison fort. Finds have been too few to postulate a chronology: the fortlet was equipped with a stone rampart, and whilst occupation from the Flavian period is not ruled out by the finds, a second-century foundation seems more likely.

Alongside the temporary camps and permanent forts across Stainmore, there is also a series of signal—or watch—towers, three on Stainmore itself, if we include Maiden Castle.[38] Bowes Moor and Roper Castle are closely comparable oblong earthworks. In recent years, however, it has been shown[39] that the system extended

14

into the western approaches to Stainmore in the form of earthworks made up of a bank with a four-post tower protected by two ditches. Sites observed and part-tested are Punchbowl Inn, Augill Bridge, Augill Castle, Appleby Golf Course and Johnson's Plain. It was suggested that the close proximity of these sites one to the other was due to the frequent poor visibility in the area. There is at present no conclusive evidence by which to date the system, although it is hard to believe that it can be later than the end of the first century.

As has already been noted, the Stainmore and north–south roads meet at Brougham: the rectangular earthwork of the Roman fort is plainly visible. However, whilst there is little dating evidence for the site, it is hardly conceivable that this important road-junction site does not go back to Agricola.[40]

From Brougham, the main north–south route follows the modern A6 closely. Just north of Penrith lies the fort of Old Penrith: a relatively extensive excavation in 1977–78 produced evidence which suggested that the fort came into operation in the post-Agricolan period, although it must be borne in mind that the excavation was largely concerned with the *vicus* on the south side of the fort, and that it may therefore be premature to infer too much from it about the history of the fort itself.[41] There are at least three other sites in the close vicinity which have been identified from the air. One of these is probably a marching-camp, although the other two, though likely military, are of uncertain type. Excavation has suggested that occupation of one of these latter does not begin until the second century.[42]

Plate 7   Brougham: the fort is visible as a playing-card shaped earthwork, with the castle in the north-west corner

Plate 8 Carlisle: the Agricolan timber gateway, showing the remains of the central post and thresholds

Plate 9 Carlisle: coins of Vespasian's reign from the interior of the Agricolan fort

A number of sites have been located in the vicinity of the road north to Carlisle: at least two marching-camps lie astride the road; also a tilery at Scalesceugh which was producing material from the first to the fourth century.[43] Of the presumed forts, Park House is now regarded as a farmstead,[44] whilst both Wreay Hall and Barrock Fell are almost certainly fortlets of considerably later date.[45]

Despite the large amounts of Roman material collected in Carlisle over the years, it is only since the early 1970s that the city has seen a large and continuous excavation programme. Roman occupation of many periods has been revealed,[46] but the earliest (Agricolan) material comes from two sites separated by a quarter of a mile or more—a civilian building at Blackfriars Street and the spectacular remains of a turf-and-timber 'fort' at Annetwell Street. The distance between these two early and contemporary sites indicates the speed at which the civilian aspect of Roman Carlisle must have developed at the beginning.

The Blackfriars Street excavations revealed that Blackfriars Street was itself a Roman street in the Flavian period with typical *vicus* buildings fronting it—long, narrow strip buildings, timber-framed, and with their gable-ends facing on to the street. The type is recognised, though in a later stone-built form, at Vindolanda.

It is now evident that a major military structure lies in the Annetwell/Abbey Street area, although its nature still contains considerable puzzles.[48] This structure probably covered the area in which the medieval castle stands. There appear to be two distinct aspects to the site: in the first place, an exceptionally well-preserved turf rampart with a 'dual-carriageway' gateway, which gives on to a gravelled road laid on to a log corduroy, suggests a military site. The evidence of the gateway, of which the timbers were sufficiently well preserved to show cart-rutting, suggests that it was an Agricolan foundation—there being a virtually fresh coin of Vespasian's eighth consulship (A.D. 77–78), sealed by one of the still-preserved posts of the western guard-tower. This structure was apparently demolished either late in the Flavian period or early in the Trajanic.

Although elements of forts of later date have been found on this site (barracks, *intervallum*—road), the buildings associated with the early rampart and gateway appear to have had more of a service function—sheds, post-and-wattle features which may have had a connection with leather-tanning. A possible interpretation is that the earliest structures on the Annetwell Street site relate to a supply-depot rather than a fort, and in that case might provide a parallel for the Red House site, near Corbridge. It is further possible that a true fort exists elsewhere—perhaps represented by the massive timber platform beneath the Museum and/or, as has often been conjectured, it lies beneath the Cathedral. It is in any case evident that either in Agricolan times or later in the late first/early second centuries, Carlisle was an important site; tile-stamps of all the British legions have been recovered from the city, and a Vindolanda tablet[49] talks of the presence there of a *centurio regionarius*— a kind of District Commissioner.

That the Stanegate road, in its inception, is Agricolan is hardly to be doubted in the light of the recognition of major Agricolan sites at both Corbridge and Carlisle. What is less certain is the dating of structures along the Stanegate, *and* the western extension of it down to Kirkbride.[50] There seems little doubt that of the forts which lie between Corbridge and Carlisle, Newbrough, Chesterholm (Vindolanda), Carvoran and Old Church, Brampton, are a mixture of late Flavian and Trajanic structures,[51] as are smaller sites like Haltwhistle Burn and Throp. Nether Denton, however, *may* be Agricolan.[52] It now seems clear that, on the western extension as well as Kirkbride, the newly discovered Stanegate forts of Finglandrigg and Burgh-by-Sands are also Trajanic, as is the watch-tower beneath the Burgh-by-Sands fort.[53] We are thus left with a problem for the future in determining how much of the Stanegate between Red House and Kirkbride, apart from the road itself together with Red House and Carlisle, is actually attributable to Agricola.

Agricola's permanent forts in the North West were built largely of turf and timber: the rectangular 'playing-card' sites were protected by a turf and clay rampart which rested on a log corduroy. This rampart was often supported by a timber revetment or fence on the inside and sometimes by a complete 'box-like' enclosing fence. Outside were ditches and other obstacles. At Watercrook, for example (itself *not* an Agricolan site), between the first and second ditch was a palisade fence made probably of branches, and an earth and rubble bank. The rampart was pierced by double-carriageway gates with guard-towers, which led to a central range of buildings consisting of Headquarters, Granaries and Commandant's House, whilst the rest of the area would be occupied largely by barracks and stables.

As noted, Agricola did not intend the Stanegate as a conventional frontier, but perhaps as one of a number of east–west lines (like Stainmore Pass and the Aire Gap) which served to break up Brigantian territory into segments which could be policed. Agricola's later work was concerned with Scotland, and it was clearly his intention to subdue the whole of the British Isles. Unfortunately for him, Britain could not be viewed in isolation, and by the early 80s it was clear that troops were going to be required to defend more vital territory in Europe. In 83 or 84, Agricola was recalled, and soon after, the Legio II *Adiutrix* was taken from Chester and replaced by the Legio XX *Valeria-Victrix*. This in its turn meant the abandonment of Inchtuthil in Perthshire, the base which was vital to the holding of northern Scotland. Thus immediately upon Agricola's departure Roman arms returned to the line of the Forth and Clyde.

Tacitus saw this as a sell-out: 'Britain was completely conquered, and immediately allowed to slip'. But the decision was a realistic one, viewing the Empire as a whole, particularly since there was obviously a good deal of consolidation work to be done in Britain—not least in the Lake District which Agricola had left virtually untouched.[54]

Notes

(N.B. References to modern books and articles are given in an abbreviated form; these references are itemised in full in the Bibliography.)

1. *Agricola*, 16–17; *Histories* III, 45; *Annals* XII, 40. The latter two are set out in full as Appendix 1.
2. Richmond (1954); cf. Hartley (1980).

3. Tacitus, *Agricola*, 8; and Statius, *Silvae* V, **2**, 31–47.
4. Jones, G. D. B. (1968), 2; Jones, M. J. (1975), 178 (Templeborough); *Britannia* IX (1978), 420 ff (Chesterfield).
5. Birley, A. R. (1976).
6. *Agricola*, 9, 0.
7. Birley, A. R. (1973), 188 f.
8. See *Britannia* XII (1981), 331; and *Britannia* XIII (1982), 352, for summaries of this work.
9. *Agricola*, 20.
10. Hanson *et al.* (1979).
11. Shotter (1979), 8; Potter (1979), 356 ff.
12. *Britannia* V (1974), 412 f.
13. Webster (1970), 172.
14. Thompson (1965), 24 ff; Jones, M. J. (1975), 142; *Britannia* VII (1976), 319 ff; *Britannia* VIII (1977), 385 ff
15. Jones, G. D. B. (1968), 6, 13.
16. Jones, G. D. B. (1972); Jones, M. J. (1975), 170 f.
17. Bruton (1909); *JRS* 56 (1966), 200.
18. Jones, G. D. B. (1974), 23 f; *Britannia* VII (1976), 319; *Britannia* XI (1980), 364; *Britannia* XII (1981), 331; *Britannia* XIII (1982), 352.
19. *Britannia* XII (1981), 331.
20. Jones, M. J. (1975), 159.
21. *Britannia* XIII (1982), 352.
22. *JRS* 54 (1964), 157; Bruton (1908).
23. Jones, M. J. (1975), 166 f.
24. Jones and Wild (1970).
25. Jones, M. J. (1975), 149.
26. Jones, G. D. B. (1970), 3.
27. Birley, E. B. (1946); Hildyard (1954).
28. *Britannia* VI (1975), 239; *Britannia* VII (1976), 319.
29. *Britannia* III (1972), 312 f.
30. Shotter (1979).
31. Birley, E. B. (1946), 145.
32. Birley, E. B. (1947); Hildyard (1951).
33. Hildyard (1951), 53 f; cf. Potter (1979), 356 f.
34. For Rey Cross and Crackenthorpe, see Richmond and McIntyre (1934); for Kirkby Thore, see *Britannia* X (1979), 283; for Plumpton Head, see *Britannia* VI (1975), 232 f.
35. Charlesworth (1964).
36. *JRS* 58 (1968), 179 f.
37. Birley, E. B. (1958); Jones, M. J. (1977).
38. Richmond (1951).
39. Higham and Jones (1975).
40. Birley, E. B. (1932).
41. *Britannia* IX (1978), 424 f.
42. St. Joseph (1951); Poulter (1982).
43. *Britannia* II (1971), 251.
44. Bellhouse (1954a); Higham and Jones (1975), 34.
45. Bellhouse (1953); Collingwood (1931).
46. McCarthy (1980).
47. *Britannia* IX (1978), 423; *Britannia* X (1979), 281.
48. *Britannia* V (1974), 410 f; *Britannia* IX (1978), 421 ff; *Britannia* X (1979), 281.
49. Bowman and Thomas (1983), Document No. 22.
50. Bellhouse and Richardson (1982).
51. Breeze and Dobson (1976), 20 ff.
52. Jones, M. J. (1975), 169.
53. *Britannia* X (1979), 281 ff; Jones, G. D. B. (1982), 284 f.
54. Hartley (1966), 12.

3

Consolidation, A.D. 83–120

The period between Agricola's departure from Britain in A.D. 83 or 84 and the building of Hadrian's Wall in the 120s is one of the less well-known episodes in Romano–British history. Yet is contains not only the events that led up to the building of Britain's best-known Roman relic, but also the complete withdrawal from Scotland. For this period, therefore, we are more than ever reliant on scraps of literary information, together with the evidence of inscriptions, and the interpretation of numismatic, ceramic and stratigraphic evidence from the sites themselves.

Tacitus published his biography of Agricola in A.D. 98, two years after the death of the emperor Domitian, about whom the historian was less than enthusiastic; it is clear that he held Domitian as having been maliciously responsible for the fact that Agricola obtained no further post of responsibility after Britain; and there is more than a hint that the Emperor may not have been entirely free of having had a hand in Agricola's death in A.D. 93 at the early age of 53. It is hardly likely, therefore, that Tacitus can be regarded as an entirely unbiased source for the events of Domitian's reign.

At the opening of his *Histories*,[1] five Latin words sum up the Flavian achievement in Britain, as Tacitus saw it: 'Britain was totally conquered, and immediately let slip'. In a sense, we can confirm Tacitus' judgement by noting the situation at Agricola's departure, where the Caledonians had been defeated at Mons Graupius (possibly near the shores of the Moray Firth), and where there seemed no further enemy left—except the terrain: with it we may compare the extremely cryptic reference by Spartianus, the biographer of Hadrian,[2] to the fact that at the time of Trajan's death in the East in A.D. 117, 'the Britons could not be kept under Roman control'. Between these two dates we know that one of Agricola's successors in Britain, Sallustius Lucullus, was executed allegedly for having named a new type of lance after himself:[3] since this happened in A.D. 89 it is likely that it was not unconnected with a serious rebellion on the Rhine, instigated by one Antonius Saturninus. Further, the poet Juvenal in a Satire about Domitian's court[4] mentions hopes of capturing Arviragus of the Britons—obviously a name of some significance to find a place in a work intended for a Roman audience. He also refers in another Satire[5] to soldiers 'blooding' themselves in battle with the Brigantes—which must presumably have a 'dramatic date' of *c*. A.D. 100.

The only other piece of documentary evidence consists of a coin of Hadrian, minted in A.D. 119 with the legend BRITANNIA,[6] which is distinct from the BRITANNIA coin issued later in the reign commemorating Hadrian's journey to Britain. The coin of A.D. 119, that is during the governorship of Q. Pompeius Falco, must surely refer to victories which must have been Hadrian's initial response to the problems alluded to by Spartianus.

The most tangible change in the situation in Britain over this forty-year period was of course the withdrawal from Scotland. The first stage of this—from the Moray

Firth to the line of the Forth and the Clyde can reasonably be dated to *c.* A.D. 86–87 on the evidence of demolition at Agricola's legionary base at Inchtuthil. The cause of this was undoubtedly in part the growing troubles on the Danube; these necessitated the withdrawal of a legion from the uncompleted fortress at Inchtuthil, which in its turn meant that the heart had gone from Agricola's northern Scottish arrangements. In any case, it could no doubt be argued that now that the Caledonians had been defeated for a generation, at least, there was no need to garrison this part of Scotland and territory south of the Forth–Clyde line would be left unmolested to Romanise. That this was viewed positively can be seen from the decision to rebuild Agricola's key site of Newstead (Roxburghshire) on a larger scale in the later years of Domitian's reign.

What led to the loss of the rest of Scotland early in the second century is less clear: Juvenal's references certainly suggest disturbance on the borders, and we may assume from the decision to fortify the Stanegate, and thus strengthen its policing/frontier role, that the withdrawal was an enforced one. Indeed widespread fire damage observed on southern Scottish sites appears to confirm this. A context for this might have been further troop withdrawals as the Danube crisis deepened. However, in the absence of literary information, a precise date is elusive.

This might certainly appear to corroborate Tacitus' serious misgivings about the British situation. Fortunately, however, we have now a sufficient body of archaeological data to realise that there was definitely a positive side to this period. The Trajanic (or possibly late Flavian) work on the Stanegate itself shows that it was not intended that the rot should run any deeper. As we have seen, there were certainly two stages to this—the watch-towers and perhaps the smaller forts, followed by the series of major forts. It may be that the whole of the western extension (from Carlisle to Kirkbride) should be dated to this period, indicating the realisation of the dangers posed by the formidable nature of the Solway. Most recent research has indicated that the western Stanegate was seen as a running barrier to keep out intruders. At the same time there is clearly still a great deal to be understood about late Flavian/Trajanic frontier arrangements[7]—in particular, the large number of building phases evident at some of the sites—four, for example, in this period at Corbridge and Chesterholm (Vindolanda). At any rate, the importance of Carlisle at this stage has become very evident (see above in Chapter 2).

Thus one, perhaps the major, element of the post-Agricolan consolidation was the provision of a visible frontier to the north of the province. As we have already seen, the Lake District appears to have been the major part of North-West England which Agricola had left untouched. It is largely through critical studies of the pottery and coin-loss evidence that we have come to recognise the sites that are post-Agricolan in date. The chief forts that pierce and surround the Lake District, in addition to those Agricolan and probable Agricolan sites on the Lune and the Eden, are Old Carlisle, Papcastle, Caermote, Old Penrith, Troutbeck, Ambleside, Hardknott, Ravenglass and Watercrook: as well as these there are the coastal forts of Beckfoot, Maryport, Burrow Walls and Moresby, which will be discussed more fully in the next chapter.

Few of these have seen large-scale work: Old Carlisle, a fort with an extensive *vicus*, is virtually untouched,[8] and so no date can be assigned. Papcastle[9] has produced evidence of timber structures and material which, though not decisive, do not rule out a late Flavian date. At Caermote,[10] two turf-and-timber forts have been found, one inside the other. The larger is the earlier fort, and a Trajanic date for the larger, and a Hadrianic date for the smaller, would not be inconsistent with the evidence. The dating evidence would not appear to support the Agricolan foundation which has been argued on grounds of gateway-style.

On the eastern side of the Lakes, recent excavation at Old Penrith has argued for a date not earlier than the late Flavian period,[11] although it should be remembered that chronological coincidence between fort and *vicus* occupation should not necessarily be assumed. Brougham fort has produced no evidence, though burials in the cemetery were dated to the second and third centuries A.D.[12] At Low Borrow Bridge, as we have seen, there is some suggestion of an enlargement of the fort in the form of a pebbly-clay rampart which may have been associated with a stone wall: however, even if the interpretation is correct, dating remains hazardous, although a second-century date for the 'large' fort cannot be ruled out.[13] Between Penrith and Keswick, in the vicinity of the known marching-camp at Troutbeck, lies a newly-recognised fort site. Although not firmly dated, this fort had a rampart of clay blocks, and would fit the policing network. At some later date this fort was reduced in size.[14]

Relatively large-scale excavations were carried out at Ambleside earlier in the century, and revealed a slightly irregular rectangular fort defended by clay ramparts. Outside there were two and, in places, three ditches. The central range of buildings was uncovered, though relating to a later stone-built phase of the fort. On the basis of the pottery the foundation of the fort has been assigned to the late Flavian period.[15] It is, however, worth noting that during site clearance in 1982 approximately half a mile to the north of the fort, features were observed which would not be inconsistent with a defensive system, though associated pottery was largely second century.

Presumably as part of the policing arrangements for the Lake District, a road was eventually driven through from Ambleside to the coast at Ravenglass. Although we now know that the latter site is of Hadrianic date, the intermediate fort at Hardknott is now regarded as having a Trajanic foundation.[16] This almost square fort is superbly sited with excellent visibility down Eskdale to the sea. The fort is stone-built, although it is assumed that a rampart-bank was originally provided and it had two ditches where necessary: on parts of the site, however, natural features obviated the need to cut ditches. Excavation of interior features revealed two phases of barrack block—timber and stone.[17]

Ravenglass will be discussed more fully in its coastal context in the next chapter, but for the present purpose it is sufficient to say that the most recent excavations suggest that a mid-Hadrianic fort was preceded by an early Hadrianic fortlet on a different alignment. The dating of the other coastal forts is hazardous: Maryport, of which a stone wall and rampart have been recovered, appears on coin and pottery evidence to be a late Flavian or, more likely, Trajanic foundation.[18] Of Moresby,

Plate 10   Hardknott: the fort and bath-house

Plate 11   Hardknott: the headquarters (*principia*)

Plate 12   Hardknott: the fort's bath-house

Plate 13   Watercrook: the surviving core of the fort-wall and inner ditch

24

Burrow Walls and Beckfoot, little is known, apart from the Hadrianic building-inscription from Moresby,[19] which has prompted the plausible suggestion[20] that on the coastal system the forts may have been in general a later addition—as, of course, they were on Hadrian's Wall itself.

Further south, recent work at Watercrook,[21] although largely confined to the *vicus*, has suggested that the first phase, recognised in a clay-and-turf rampart, should not be placed earlier than late Flavian times. On the east angle, the outer defences consisted of three ditches: between the first and second was a palisade *and* a stone bank. The fort, which is nearly square, was protected on three sides by the bow of the River Kent, prompting the suggestion that it, rather than Hardknott, may be MEDIBOGDO of the *Ravenna Cosmography*—the name meaning 'Fort in the middle of a bow' which closely describes Watercrook's disposition.

Thus consolidation work in the Lake District had the effect of driving east–west policing lines from the main north–south route in the direction of the coast. Field work also suggests the linking of some of these sites by north–south roads, which would thus have the effect of imposing an informal 'grid' on the area. One unanswered question concerns the southern fringes of the Lakes: no sites have been recovered, although the volume of finds in the Cartmel and Barrow areas suggests the possible existence of sites in Furness. It is similarly possible that sites await discovery on the coastline of southern Cumbria—for example, between Moresby and Ravenglass, and between Ravenglass and Barrow. In the former case it is worth noting the substantial amount of material to come from the Beckermet area.[22]

The picture across Stainmore[23] in the consolidation period is unclear. At Greta Bridge, occupation from late Flavian times is assumed on the basis of finds, whilst at Bowes the elaborate Flavian (Agricolan) rampart was modified, though at a date not certainly proved. The fort at Brough, as noted above, has produced no clear evidence of its structural sequence, though its long-term importance is attested by the large collection of lead sealings of various army units found there. Kirkby Thore certainly had a second phase turf-and-clay rampart, though its date is uncertain.

Further south, other Pennine routes received attention: the probably Agricolan fort at Long Preston, a six-acre structure defended by a turf rampart, was at an unspecified time replaced by a smaller (three-acre) fort, also defended by a turf rampart.[24] Castleshaw, too, was reduced in size—the Agricolan fort of three acres being replaced by one of 0·6 acres built inside the earlier one: whilst the second fort was undoubtedly second century, the exact date of its foundation is unclear.[25] The changes of size, noted here and elsewhere in the North West, must surely indicate considerable garrison modifications—a problem which will be examined further below.

Whilst consolidation in Cumbria basically meant the laying out of a new fort-system, the military framework of Lancashire and Cheshire already existed. At Burrow-in-Lonsdale it appears that the presumed Agricolan turf-and-timber fort was modified and realigned, but at what date cannot be determined.[26] It is not unreasonable, however, to assume that a fair life-span for a turf-and-timber fort might be twenty to twenty-five years before major modification and repair were required. In

25

this case, provided that there was not a break in occupation at Burrow, a Trajanic date for the modifications would seem reasonable.

At the mouth of the Lune, Lancaster too underwent modification; in this case, a Trajanic building inscription[27] gives a clear indication and is presumably to be associated with the clay rampart and stone wall resting on a bevelled plinth course observed to the north of the Old Vicarage. As noted above, this line of defence represented an enlargement of the earliest fort. Similarly, traces of the eastern gateway of a stone fort were excavated at the junction of Church Street and the passage of the road through the gateway.

The Ribble forts also underwent modification. The addition of a stone wall to the first-phase rampart at Kirkham could conceivably be Trajanic.[28] At Ribchester, the evident complication of the site makes interpretation more difficult. The recent discovery of a previously unknown defence system[29] suggests the existence of a second turf-and-timber fort, which had perhaps been turned through 90 degrees, possibly indicating an enlargement and a change of garrison type. If so, it is likely that both these phases are Flavian—though on present evidence whether that should be interpreted as Agricolan and post-Agricolan or pre-Agricolan and Agricolan is not easy to determine. A stone wall was later added to the front of the rampart, although again a precise date is not easy to assign; there is nothing against its being

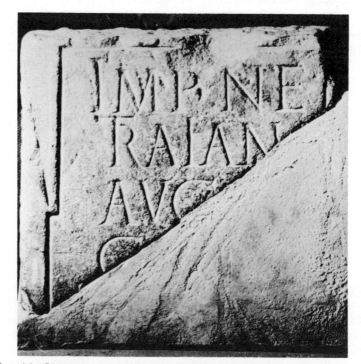

Plate 14   Lancaster: part of a stone building; inscription of Trajan's reign

of Trajanic date,[30] although the visible stone buildings (that is, the granaries) are more likely Severan.[31]

At Manchester, recent excavations[32] have demonstrated two turf-and-timber phases, the later of the two representing an enlargement of the fort from approximately four to five acres, apparently early in the second century. The mid-second century saw the addition of a stone wall to the later rampart. The same structural sequence has been observed both in the western defences and in the area of the north gateway. Further south at Northwich, two phases of fort were recognised—an Agricolan phase which lasted until early in the second century, which was followed by the building of a wall to the front of the rampart. The commencement date of phase II was not precisely placed, but may well be Trajanic: further, this second-phase fort (and, with it, military occupation at Northwich) seems to have ended contemporaneously with the Antonine advance into Scotland in the 140s. The site's later industrial activity will be discussed below.

Excavations of the legionary fortress at Chester have shown that it, too, shared in the work of consolidation: as noted above, the original fortification of Chester clearly goes back to Neronian times, but the Abbey Green excavations showed that the Flavian fortress itself underwent a number of modifications before the Trajanic rebuilding in stone.[33]

Thus it can be seen that in Lancashire and Cheshire the consolidation period represented a chronologically fairly uniform process of rebuilding and often enlarging Agricola's forts early in the Trajanic period; this fact incidentally can be regarded as confirmation of Tacitus' observation about Agricola's good eye for fort placement.[34]

It is stated by Tacitus that the results of Agricola's campaigns in their effects on the native population were dramatic—in terms of the abandonment of hostility and the acceptance of garrisons.[35] This certainly implies a rapid establishment of peace: in a sense, the growth outside the forts of civilian settlements (vici) which were presumably in the main undefended tends to confirm this. It can be shown (see below) that the majority of the forts saw vici established very soon after their own initial foundation. We also find that the manufacture and provision of building and other materials for the army, which was initially established perhaps on an ad hoc basis were, during the consolidation period, centralised. Whilst the evidence of industrial sites will be discussed more fully later, it is certainly relevant to the present purpose that individual manufacturing sites such as Holt (for Chester), Quernmore (for Lancaster), Muncaster (for Hardknott/Ravenglass), Brampton (for Old Church, Brampton), and Scalesceugh[36] were perhaps at least partly superseded by the growth of much larger manufacturing and supply centres—for example, Wilderspool, which appears to have started in the late Flavian/Trajanic period,[37] and Walton-le-Dale. As will be shown later, there is a good deal of reason to suppose that Wilderspool at any rate relied on native workers: the same may perhaps be said of 'industrial areas' within the vici: work at Manchester, Northwich and Middlewich has produced evidence of industrial activity in close connection with military sites. Whilst it may be the case at Northwich and Middlewich that this work followed military evacuation, at Manchester the 'industrial estate' was clearly part of the vicus and contemporary with the fort.[38] At the latter site, the movement of suitable raw materials to the site itself certainly implies settled conditions, possibly over a considerable area.[39]

However, whilst the work of Agricola and his successors certainly represents overall a positive achievement, and whilst, as we have seen, there is evidence which implies settled conditions, it is nonetheless true that the military could not afford to relax: a tight 'policing' network had been constructed, although this could of course break down, particularly in areas where movement was difficult. As we have seen, the evidence of field work and excavation, combined with the comment of Spartianus, shows that conditions in the north of the region in the early second century had become tense and dangerous—perhaps because of further troop withdrawals in connection with Trajan's Dacian and Parthian wars. It is certainly evident that Hadrian's reappraisal in A.D. 117 showed him that the Trajanic level of military momentum was neither desirable nor practicable. Further, there is some evidence from early imperial coin-hoards in Lancashire[40] that conditions had become less settled in the south of the region also.

It is clear that Hadrian 'stopped the rot'—initially by intervention through his governor, Q. Pompeius Falco. The longer-term and more radical solution, which may in fact be regarded as the culmination of consolidation, was the building of a new frontier—this time not a road, but a continuous barrier—Hadrian's Wall.

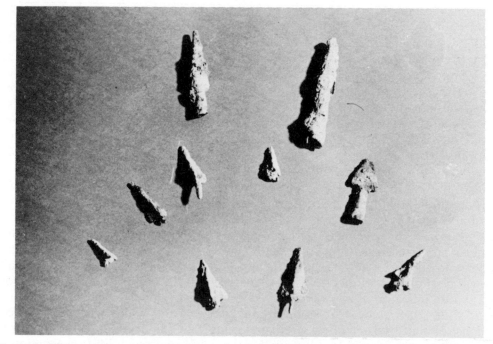

Plate 15   Watercrook: weapons (arrow- and spear-heads) recovered from the fort ditches (photograph by J. Thompson)

28

Notes

(N. B. References to modern books and articles are given in an abbreviated form; these references are itemised in full in the Bibliography.)

1. *Histories* I, 2. The *Histories* were published *c.* A.D. 106.
2. *Scriptores Historiae Augustae* (SHA), *Hadrianus* 5, 2; the writers of the Augustan History produced biographies of emperors of the second and third centuries; these are of varying reliability, although Spartianus is *not* amongst the worst.
3. Suetonius, *Domitian* 10.
4. *Satires* IV, 127.
5. *Satires* XIV, 196.
6. Hill (1970), 53.
7. Breeze and Dobson (1976), 20ff.
8. Birley, E. B. (1951).
9. Birley, E. B. (1963); Charlesworth (1965).
10. Bellhouse (1960a); Jones, M. J. (1975), 135.
11. *Britannia* IX (1978), 424f.
12. *JRS* 57 (1967), 177; *JRS* 58 (1968), 179.
13. Jones, M. J. (1975), 164.
14. Jones, M. J. (1975), 180.
15. Hartley (1966), 12.
16. Potter (1979), 48f (Ravenglass); Hartley (1966), 12 (Hardknott).
17. *JRS* 55 (1965), 203; Jones, M. J. (1975), 154f.
18. Jarrett (1976).
19. *RIB* 801; the inscription is dated to post-A.D. 128.
20. Potter (1979), 359.
21. Potter (1979).
22. Shotter (1980), 163.
23. Jones, M. J. (1975), 154 (Greta Bridge); Jones, M. J. (1975), 130f (Bowes); Richmond (1936) (Brough); Jones, M. J. (1975), 158 (Kirkby Thore).
24. Jones, M. J. (1975), 162f.
25. Jones, M. J. (1975), 140.
26. Jones, M. J. (1975), 134.
27. *RIB* 604.
28. Jones, M. J. (1975), 159.
29. *Britannia* XII (1981), 331.
30. Edwards (1972), 6; Jones, M. J. (1975), 175.
31. Jones, G. D. B. (1970), 239; for the structural sequence, see *Britannia* X (1979), 291f.
32. *Britannia* XI (1980), 364; *Britannia* XIII (1982), 353.
33. *RIB* 464; *Britannia* IX (1978), 429f.
34. *Agricola*, 22.
35. *Agricola*, 20.
36. Grimes (1930) (Holt); *Britannia* II (1971), 254 (Quernmore); Bellhouse (1960b) (Muncaster); Hogg (1965) (Brampton); *Britannia* II (1971), 251 (Scalesceugh).
37. Thompson (1965), 67–87.
38. Jones, G. D. B. (1974).
39. Jones, G. D. B. (1974), 153f.
40. Shotter (1978b).

4
The Northern Frontier

The events in the northern frontier area in the first two decades of the second century are, as we have seen, riddled with interpretative problems. The only certain element is that there was disturbance—possibly throughout the whole of the North West. It seems that this trouble had first to be dealt with, and then a more lasting answer found to it. By inference we can assume that Hadrian's view was that, alone, the Stanegate system was inadequate.

Hadrian himself came to Britain in A.D. 121 or 122—evidently almost the first of his long series of imperial visits.[1] Apart from the introduction of a new policy, two further, presumably related, changes may be discerned: the governor Q. Pompeius Falco was replaced by A. Platorius Nepos (A.D. 122–125), and Legio IX *Hispana* at York was replaced by Legio VI *Victrix*, previously garrisoned at Vetera on the Rhine. Nepos' earlier career had given him service as governor of Lower Germany, whilst the legion must have had extensive experience of frontier works on the Rhine (*Limes Germanicus*), and it has been suggested[2] that the legion came straight from the Rhine to the Tyne. Although Legio IX *Hispana* had not over the years had a happy time in Britain and may well have suffered in the recent disturbances, the embroidered story of its disappearance is romantic fiction. That the new policy was Hadrian's own is attested by his biographer, Spartianus: 'He made for Britain, where he set right many things and—the first to do so—drew a wall along a length of eighty miles to separate barbarians and Romans'.

Recent treatments obviate the need for a *detailed* discussion of the Wall: comment will thus be restricted to more general observations. It is evident that in the first instance Hadrian's Wall was seen as a unity with the Stanegate, since although small patrols (perhaps approximately twenty men each) were housed in the Milecastles, the main bodies of troops at first remained in the Stanegate forts. Whilst the Stanegate ran through the valleys of the Tyne, Irthing and Eden rivers, the Wall occupied the northern crests of those valleys. In all, then, this will have had the effect of retaining the policing potential of the traditional *limes* and added to it the ability both to see and deal with threats from the north. It was thus in effect a 'barrier-*limes*' that cut through northern Brigantian territory, controlling traffic and the inter-connection of groups whose combination we must assume to have been considered hazardous. The Wall, with the enormous strategic advantage it must have gained from such natural features as the Great Whin Sill, will have greatly enhanced the policing potential of the Stanegate since it will have relieved pressure from the northern flank of that line.

The original Wall plan seems to have included the Wall itself, a ditch to the north (not cut where natural features made it unnecessary), and milecastles each Roman mile, between each pair of which were two square turrets. With installations so thickly laid down, lateral communications along the Wall were clearly at a premium. The Wall eventually ran from Wallsend in the east to Bowness-on-Solway in the west; its eastern two-thirds (as far as the Irthing Gap) were built of stone, whilst the western third was of turf, with installations of turf and timber construction. A fragmentary wooden inscription from Milecastle 50 places this work in Nepos' governorship.

The reason for the change in building-materials on the western sector has often been discussed—with various solutions proposed. Possibly it was the paucity of good building-stone, at least close enough at hand to make quarrying a worthwhile and/or safe undertaking. This might be of relevance if, as many have supposed, the chief problems with local tribesmen lay in the west. We should, however, remember that for most of the occupation of the north to that time, turf and timber had been regarded as perfectly adequate materials: we should not therefore necessarily assume that in the Roman mind the materials of the western sector were markedly inferior in capability to the stone of the east. The chief problem would be a longer-term one—namely, that the turf and timber would presumably require renovation before the stonework.

Platorius Nepos was replaced as governor in A.D. 125 or 126; at about this time the decision was evidently made to bring the main bodies of troops on to the Wall itself and to build forts for them there. Recent excavation at Bowness-on-Solway[3] has suggested that the process may not have been chronologically uniform over the entire Wall, and certainly Carrawburgh, by its relationship with the *Vallum*, can be shown to be an 'after thought' (*c.* A.D. 133). In effect, therefore, the Stanegate forts of Chesterholm (Vindolanda), Nether Denton and Brampton were advanced to House-steads, Great Chesters, Birdoswald and Castlesteads, whilst at Carvoran the Wall

Plate 16   Housesteads: the granaries

and the Stanegate were close enough for the fort to be retained. At Carlisle, a new fort was built at Stanwix, although recent excavation suggests that this did not mean the loss of a garrison at Carlisle itself. On the western Stanegate, Burgh I, Finglandrigg, and Kirkbride were advanced respectively to Burgh II, Drumburgh and Bowness-on-Solway. The relationship between the 'fort phase' and the 'pre-fort phase' had been convincingly demonstrated by the discovery that some of the forts overlie already existing Wall installations—for example, at Housesteads.[4] We should also note that in the western sector (except at Birdoswald) the turf wall was supplied with turf-and-timber forts.

To the south of the forts, and evidently part of the same plan, ran the *Vallum*, the name used for the feature since Bede's time. This consisted of a flat-bottomed ditch, some 8 feet deep, with steep sides. When kept clean, it would have been extremely hard for an intruder to extricate himself from it: north and south of the *Vallum*-ditch were cleared areas (or berms), bounded by continuous mounds of earth made up of the upcast from the ditch and carefully revetted with turf. The feature, which runs the whole length of the Wall on its southern side (except for the eastern extension to Wallsend) was 120 feet wide overall. Its purpose has been much discussed, but it would appear to demarcate a military zone on the southern side of the Wall, and probably act as a 'man-trap'—thus either keeping out unauthorised people or getting them into a position where they would not easily be able to get across to the north of the Wall, and perhaps trap them until they were rounded-up by patrols.

The *Vallum* may perhaps give us a clue as to why the 'fort-phase' of the Wall was undertaken: a military zone which consisted of the Wall, the Stanegate and inter-vening territory was perhaps too wide in most areas for convenience or efficiency as well as security. For example, the distance between Kirkbride and its 'Wall-equivalent', Bowness-on-Solway, is four miles. In this connection, it is worth noting that even in a communications role the Stanegate was superseded by the Military Way which ran in the Wall/*Vallum* corridor.

The whole system was thus in place by the mid-130s, and it is suggested[5] that the replacement of turf by stone structures began late in Hadrian's reign, but may not have been completed until after the evacuation of the Antonine Wall in the early 160s. Three outpost forts were provided to the north of the Wall—at Birrens, Netherby and Bewcastle. It is argued[6] that these were not 'early-warning' forts, but placed to protect that part of Brigantian territory which was cut off by the Wall—an argument which receives some force from the discovery of the *Brigantia* relief at Birrens. It is further argued that since these forts are tied to Hadrian's Wall by a road, which runs to Milecastle 50 rather than to Birdoswald, they were part of the original *plan*, though not necessarily actually built until the mid-Hadrianic period. Notable amongst these is Bewcastle, which abandons the normal rectangular shape in favour of an irregular polygon encompassing a hill-top: this was presumably intended to give it good visibility in what might be expected to be troubled terrain.

The wall-forts were all of a size to accommodate complete units.[7] The average acreage is approximately five, with the two largest at Bowness-on-Solway (7) and Stanwix (9.32). Despite some confusions over the names of Hadrian's Wall forts,[8] there seems no doubt that Stanwix housed the milliary *Ala Petriana*, and was the Wall's command centre—a point which receives added weight from its close proximity to Carlisle, where recent excavation has shown a continued military presence in the second century, and has revealed evidence for the presence there of detachments at least of all three British legions. It has been calculated that the Wall installations will in all have required around 11,500 men: this will obviously have required some movement of garrisons from existing bases, but this will be treated more fully later.

Hadrian's successor, Antoninus Pius, once again initiated a forward policy: his views may reflect a gradually more insecure situation in southern Scotland, or the desire to make southern Scotland more of a barrier against the real enemy in the north. Further, as a relatively unknown senator, he may have, like Claudius, felt the need to bolster his military reputation. A detailed study of the Antonine Wall[9] would clearly be out of place in the present volume: it will thus be treated only in so far as it affected the situation in northern England.

The removal of the armies northwards came in A.D. 143 under the governor, Q. Lollius Urbicus, and possibly in response to some pressure on the northern frontier.[10] It is clear enough that this entailed the substantial decommissioning of Hadrian's Wall, for Hartley's study of the Samian ware from both Walls shows that they were not held contemporaneously; it has been shown, for example, that the *Vallum* ditch was filled with turf to make it easy to cross. At the same time it has long been recognised that some, at least, of the Antonine Wall forts enjoyed two periods of occupation.[11] It now seems clear—and the numismatic evidence can be shown to support this[12]—that the two periods have to be seen within a shorter time-span than has traditionally been the case.

It is evident that the first period ended, probably violently, *c.* A.D. 155: it is likely that Antoninus' 'dejected' BRITANNIA coin of A.D. 154–5 reflects this. It is now reasonable to assume that the second period was brief, and probably a 'punitive' measure launched by Marcus Aurelius on his accession and terminated as soon as it had achieved its objectives—perhaps *c.*A.D. 163. The circumstances of this are not clear, though disturbance in the north must be assumed, and indeed, as will be seen, evidently continued intermittently throughout the rest of the second century. However, the notion of a major Brigantian revolt during Antoninus' reign has recently been challenged.[13]

The existence of Roman installations on the coast of Cumbria has long been known; however, the questions of their extent, complexity and evolution have been the subject of a great deal of research and debate in recent years—both on the ground and from the air.[14]

A concentrated period since the mid-1950s of aerial reconnaissance, ground-work and mainly relatively small-scale excavation has revealed the existence on the coastline westward from Bowness-on-Solway of a series of auxiliary forts, fortlets every Roman mile and two towers between each pair of milefortlets: besides which, there is evidence of linear features in the form of a road with side ditches and palisades. The most complete excavations to have taken place so far are on Milefortlets 1 (Biglands) and 5 (Cardurnock), and Tower 4B (Cardurnock).[15]

Jones' excavations at Tower 4B have come closest to showing a developmental sequence for a coastal defence arrangement; the stages appear to be: (I) a palisade or fence, fronted by a ditch and having along it, regularly spaced between each pair of milefortlets, small 'towers' of clay and turf construction. A road ran to the rear of this; (II) a new palisade, slightly inland of the first, which cut through the period I 'tower'. This, too, was associated with a road; (III) absence of a running barrier, and re-siting of a stone-built 'tower' nearer the sea and overlying the ditch of period I.

Features comparable to these have been located further south at Silloth;[16] here were located two palisades, running north–south though not quite parallel to each other, and two ditches representing the flanking ditches of a north–south coastal road. The palisades consisted of a trench packed with clay into which at close intervals double posts had been pushed. It is assumed that these posts supported wattle sections, and that the whole can be seen to fit a description of Hadrianic frontiers to be found in Spartianus' biography:[17] 'During this period, and frequently at other times, in a great many places where the barbarians are separated off not by rivers but by frontier-barriers, he set them apart by great stakes driven deep into the ground, and fastened together in the manner of a palisade'.

This description, which has usually been taken to apply to arrangements in Germany, but which clearly, from the above text, is not meant to be limited to one area alone, can be seen to have obvious relevance to the palisades located on the coast of Cumbria.

How far along the coast similar arrangements exist is hard to say, but it is clear that different areas show evidence of different treatment: for example, running towards Milefortlet 1 (Biglands) from the east, are two ditches which diverge to join the north and south ditches of the milefortlet. It is assumed that these ditches, therefore, provided a corridor in which the coastal installations were located.[18] Further research, however, has suggested that from Milefortlet 3 (Pasture House), or possibly Milefortlet 2 (North Plain), only a single forward ditch was cut.[19] It is also clear that since Milefortlet 1 (Biglands) is in excess of a *Roman* mile to the west of Bowness-on-Solway, the two systems (that is, Hadrian's Wall and the Coastal System) were not planned in complete conjunction.

The excavation of Milefortlet 1 (Biglands) has demonstrated a sequence of three periods[20]—a sequence which has been shown to be compatible with other milefortlet sites where excavation has taken place. Owing to the sparse nature of the dating evidence, these three periods have to be asserted rather tentatively, apart from the fact that all fall within the second century A.D. It is reasonably certain that Phase I should be placed in the period *c*. A.D. 125–140, thus corresponding approximately with the building and first Antonine abandonment of Hadrian's Wall. Given the new, but now generally accepted, sequence on the Antonine Wall,[21] there is no objection to Phase II of Biglands being placed between Antonine Wall I and II, with Phase III of Biglands commencing *c*. A.D. 163 and extending until *c*. A.D. 180 (or possibly *c*. A.D. 200). At a number of the coastal installation, three phases have been detected, and at none is the dating evidence inconsistent with Potter's conclusions concerning Biglands. Further it is probably not unreasonable to relate the three

Plate 17 Biglands: the first milefortlet of the coastal system showing as a crop-mark just below the farm buildings (photograph by T. W. J. Potter)

Plate 18 Beckfoot: the fort and ditches show as crop-marks (photograph by T. W. J. Potter)

phases of the milefortlet with the three phases detected in connection with the barrier and tower at 4B (Cardurnock; see above).

The character of the milefortlets so far examined varies: it would appear that with the certain exception of Milefortlet 5 (Cardurnock: 1,130 m²) and possibly also of Milefortlet 9 (Skinburness)[22] which are larger than average, the milefortlets' areas are approximately 300–350m² in each case—that is, capable of holding a small patrol group. The larger ones are presumably to be explained on the basis of their special positions which required larger than normal garrisons—perhaps a *centuria*. Although it cannot be said that the rest all conform to a similar structural pattern, it would appear that they have turf-and-clay ramparts, defended by a palisade and a single ditch. They are entered front and rear by six-post timber gateways. Inside, the buildings appear to be of a rather ephemeral character; perhaps rather like turf-and-timber sheds with cooking facilities clearly apparent.

Phases I and II were closely similar, although separated by deliberate demolition. Phase III, however, was considerably smaller, and the rampart pierced by an entrance, rather than a gateway. Similar reductions and deteriorations have been observed elsewhere than at Biglands. It is also worth noting that the evidence of a small fortlet beneath the later Hadrianic fort at Ravenglass suggests a structure not dissimilar in size to Biglands.[23]

The auxiliary forts on the coast have similarly produced little evidence for their construction dates and subsequent chronology. Beckfoot and Burrow Walls give us no basis for speculation: Moresby at least has a Hadrianic building inscription of post-A.D. 128.[24] Excavation at Ravenglass suggests strongly a late Hadrianic date for initial occupation of the fort. Maryport, on the other hand, on the basis of the 1966 excavations[25] has been given a Hadrianic foundation date, although it has been pointed out[26] that the finds would support an earlier—perhaps late Flavian—date. It has been suggested, as on Hadrian's Wall itself, that the auxiliary forts represent a revision of the original plan,[27] although that does not preclude the possibility that one at least (Maryport) predated the rest of the system.

A further problem concerns the overall extent of the coastal system: the generally accepted enumeration presupposes that the defences were continuous from Bowness-on-Solway, that is, that they skirted round *Moricambe*—an assumption that has in fact no support in the evidence. Indeed it may be more likely that the defences were conceived in two parts—north and south of *Moricambe*.

The traditional view has been that the coastal system extended as far south as St Bees Head—a view which has achieved apparent support from the discovery of a probable new milefortlet at Harrington Parks,[28] which has a sight of St Bees. Bellhouse, on the other hand, has argued that, in view of the changing coastline south of Maryport, the tower at Rise How should be regarded as the southern terminus. Yet again, Potter, arguing from the existence of the fortlet beneath the fort at Ravenglass, has suggested that the system may continue much further south than is often thought. A compromise might be suggested. It has been shown that the hinterland from Carlisle to Maryport had very substantial native settlement, which, it might be argued, required defending from those seeking to pillage or destroy. Clearly, this risk lessens as the coastline starts to provide a greater natural defence; an occasional watchtower might be sufficient. We might therefore expect to find further sections of defence where the coast merited it, and where the hinterland supported substantial settlement. The lower reaches of the Esk to its estuary at Ravenglass might be regarded as such an area. Further areas could be postulated, and in considering both this and the possibility of sites lost to coastal change, we have to remember that high-tide level on the west coast was considerably higher in the Roman period than it is now.[29]

In short, therefore, we are beginning to see progress on all three of the initial questions posed concerning the coastal system—its extent, complexity and evolution. The first of these requires more work, whilst the other two, although presenting a clear enough picture for the second century, are further complicated by a limited amount of fourth-century evidence—which we shall consider below.

The provision of the Stanegate fortifications, then Hadrian's Wall and the coastal system, and then the Antonine Wall, must clearly have necessitated great flexibility in troop disposition in the north. In this matter our lack of detailed chronologies for so many sites severely hampers discussion. It is clear that some of the construction and perhaps garrison duties could be, and were, undertaken by the legions. It is similarly clear that in broad terms the Stanegate forts lost their garrisons when Hadrian's Wall was built, although this cannot be taken as a rigid feature, since the *Notitia Dignitatum*[30] in its Wall section includes Chesterholm (*Vindolanda*), a Stanegate fort. Further, we have seen that Hadrian's Wall and the coastal system were *not* held contemporaneously with the Antonine Wall.[31] These factors will certainly have aided the problems of providing garrisons for the frontier arrangements.

It is also known that at some stage in the second half of the second century, following Marcus Aurelius' Danube wars, Sarmatian troops were sent to reinforce the garrisons in Britain.[32] At least some of these were in garrison at Ribchester. Further, from Hadrian's time onwards, it was a growing practice to supplement the regular legions and auxiliary *cohortes* and *alae* with irregular units from border areas which are generally known as *numeri* and *cunei*. Of course, for sites where a sufficient body of evidence has been recovered we can sometimes see characteristic fluctuations in the ceramic and numismatic evidence to indicate temporary abandonments or reductions. It is reasonably clear, for example, that Ribchester lost its garrison when Hadrian's Wall was built, as did Lancaster, to facilitate Antoninus' advance into Scotland.[33] Some Pennine forts (such as Castleshaw and Brough-on-Noe) may have lost their garrisons.

It has been postulated that a number of sites may have seen reductions or losses of garrisons in the Trajanic/Hadrianic period: for example, Ambleside, Watercrook, Lancaster, Maryport, Kirkby Thore.[34] Further, the evidence of building sequences and of Samian pottery from Watercrook strongly indicates that the fort was being built in stone when the Antonine advance into Scotland began, was then abandoned, and reoccupied following the final withdrawal from Scotland *c*. A.D. 163. Epigraphic evidence further suggests (in the form of building inscriptions of the governorship of Calpurnius Agricola, A.D. 163–166) that Ribchester and Hardknott[35] were being rebuilt at this stage, from which we might reasonably infer garrison loss or reduction in connection with the second-century frontier movements.

In these few sites for which we have some evidence, we probably see the 'tip of the iceberg' of the Roman army's flexibility. Units could easily be moved: and it is quite likely, in view of the number of very small sites on Hadrian's Wall and the coastal system, *and*, as is now emerging,[36] on the Antonine Wall, too, that much of the detailed garrisoning must have been accomplished by taking small detachments from units whose main bases and headquarters' staffs remained elsewhere.

From the literary point of view, events of the later second century are ill-documented, and coin-loss figures, too (for monetary reasons), become less reliable indicators of occupation patterns. That Commodus' governor, Ulpius Marcellus (A.D. 180–185), had to resist attacks from the north, is made clear by Dio Cassius, and by Commodus' issue of coins commemorating victory in Britain.[37] Also during Commodus' reign an inscription from Carlisle[38] records the slaughter of 'a band of barbarians' by the *Ala Augusta Petriana*: further, an undated tombstone from Ambleside[39] records the death of one Flavius Romanus, who was killed by the enemy *inside* his fort.

The death of Commodus in A.D. 192 ushered in a period of civil war and confusion during which the governor, Clodius Albinus (A.D. 191–196), used elements of the British garrison to further his own ambitions: the result was predictable for we find his successor, Virius Lupus (A.D. 197–201) having to buy off the northern tribes and being heavily involved in rebuilding in the Pennines[40]—whether following destruction or abandonment is hard to say, though the archaeological evidence from Ravenglass[41] certainly supports enemy attack at this time followed by immediate rebuilding. Continuing building work on the frontier and in the hinterland under the Severan governors, Pudens and Senecio (A.D. 202–208) suggests continuing pressure from the north—which eventually brought the emperor himself to Britain to campaign in the north-east of Scotland. The events of the last quarter of the second century seem also to have led, as we have seen, to the decision to abandon most, if not all, of the smaller installations of the coastal system, presumably partly because they were no longer relevant (or perhaps capable), and partly because their manpower may well have been required elsewhere.

Severus and his family based themselves at York for what was clearly intended to be the final solution to the long years of disturbance. It is clear that the chief trouble lay north of the Forth/Clyde isthmus, in the shape of the Maeatae, the third-century northern neighbours of Agricola's Caledonii. Severus' campaigns took little, if any, notice of southern Scotland, nor was the Antonine Wall reoccupied. In fact it looks very like Agricola's final campaign repeated on the grand scale—perhaps hoping to take the heart of the Maeatae. Severus died at York in A.D. 211 before the work was complete, though his son and successor, Caracalla, did eventually produce a diplomatic solution which, though sneered at by ancient writers,[42] appears to have secured almost a century of peace in the north.

The garrison pattern of North-West England during the third century is difficult to establish without much more excavation:[43] in any case, the ceramic and numismatic evidence provide far less clear indications than they do for earlier periods. We may well expect that the internal upheavals which preceded Severus' rise, coupled with his own great stress on the army as the source of his power, will have led to reorganisation of existing garrisons.

The establishment of peace will have given the opportunity for more flexible handling (that is, reduction and/or movement) of garrisons. Watercrook, for example, appears to have lost its garrison early in the third century, and to have remained unmanned until the late 260s or early 270s. At Lancaster, there is evidence of substantial rebuilding in the 260s,[44] presumably following a period of abandonment. Indeed, from the Severan period through to the 240s,[45] we find a large number of sites where rebuilding was taking place. As we have seen, although the garrison pattern cannot be recovered in any detail, such evidence as there is for it, coupled with the rebuilding activity, strongly suggests large-scale redeployment. Evidently, too, there was now sufficient stability to allow for the withdrawal of garrisons from some parts of the North West.

However, as the third century wore on, as we have seen, some remanning took place. It may be assumed that the tensions experienced all over the Empire were beginning to find their expression in Britain also.

Notes

(N.B. References to modern books and articles are given in an abbreviated form; these reference are itemised in full in the Bibliography.)

1. *Scriptores Historiae Augustae (Hadrianus)* 11, 2.
2. Breeze and Dobson (1976), 54.
3. Potter (1979), 333f.
4. *JRS* 36 (1946), 134ff.
5. Breeze and Dobson (1976), 52f.
6. Breeze and Dobson (1976), 43.
7. Breeze and Dobson (1976), 48.
8. Hassall (1976); Shotter in Potter (1979), 318.
9. Robertson (1973).
10. *SHA (Antoninus)* 5, 4.
11. Breeze (1975).
12. Shotter (1976).
13. Hind (1977); Hartley (1980).
14. In particular Higham and Jones (1975); Potter (1977); Bellhouse (1981); Jones (1982).
15. Biglands (Potter, 1977); Cardurnock (Simpson and Hodgson, 1947); Tower 4B (Jones, 1982).
16. Jones (1982), 293f.
17. *SHA (Hadrianus)* 12, 6.
18. Higham and Jones (1975), 20ff.
19. Jones (1982), 287.
20. Potter (1977).
21. Breeze (1975).
22. Bellhouse (1954b), 36.
23. Potter (1979), 14ff.
24. *RIB* 801.
25. Jarrett (1976).
26. In Potter, T. W., review of Jarrett (1976), *Britannia* IX (1978), 493ff; Bellhouse (1981), 141.
27. Potter (1979), 359.

28. Jones (1982), 296.
29. Jones (1980); Jones (1982), 291 f.
30. *Occ* 40, 32 ff: the Wall section of the document is of disputed date—see Gillam (1949); also the papers in Goodburn and Bartholomew (1976).
31. Hartley (1972).
32. Dio Cassius 72, 16; narrated under A.D. 176.
33. Shotter (1979).
34. Potter (1979), 177; with individual references.
35. *RIB* 589 (Ribchester); *RIB* 793 (Hardknott).
36. Keppie and Walker (1981).
37. Dio Cassius 73, 8; for the coins, see *RIC* 440, of A.D. 183–4.
38. *RIB* 946.
39. *JRS* 53 (1963), 160.
40. Hartley (1980).
41. Dio Cassius 76, 5; Potter (1979), 363.
42. Herodian III, 15, 6.
43. Known garrisons are listed in Appendix II.
44. *RIB* 605.
45. A list of *dated* building inscriptions will be found in Appendix III.

5
Roman and Native in North-West England

Studies of Romanisation in Lowland Britain long ago demonstrated the relationship of town and country, and the way in which the economy was dominated by the Romanised tribal 'magnates'. The North West, on the other hand, was long thought to be an area with a dominant military organisation, and a quite separate and backward native population. Research over recent years has gone a long way towards demonstrating a close economic relationship between Roman and native, which it is the purpose of this chapter to discuss.

As we have seen, the disposition of the army was flexible—with auxiliary units moving as need dictated, and perhaps being split into smaller groups from time to time.[1] Increasingly, as we have seen, the regular units were supplemented or replaced by irregulars—groups of varying size and type.

The chief problems, however, in a discussion of the disposition of the army of occupation, are a basic lack of evidence,[2] and difficulties in interpreting such evidence as we have. From the *Antonine Itinerary*,[3] the *Notitia Dignitatum*[4] and the *Ravenna Cosmography*[5] we have documentation of road routes, place names and troop dispositions. But very few place names are independently attested on inscriptions from sites, which means that road routes and place names (and therefore unit dispositions) are very difficult to fix. The discovery of new stretches of roads[6] shows that we cannot yet take for granted the general directions of the Itineraries. Further, the fact that we lack detailed chronologies for most sites means that often we do not know even whether particular sites were under occupation when the routes were drawn up. It is thus possible with many of the routes to propose a number of alternative schemes[7] without even then necessarily approaching certainty.

Again with the *Notitia Dignitatum* which provides a list of sites and military units in the north, we are left with problems of dating and interpretation in the document itself;[8] yet more than this our lack of knowledge of the place names allows few positive identifications to be made. In any case few of the inscriptions from the sites themselves, which carry information about garrison-units, can be precisely dated. Thus, too often, although we know that a certain unit was in garrison at a certain site, we cannot tell when, which means in its turn that we lack the essential data to bring clarity to the *Notitia*.

However, the information that does survive in a usable form shows one essential truth—namely, that the occupation pattern was not static: garrisons were moved around, and presumably in response to changing circumstances, sites might be temporarily left without garrisons or even permanently abandoned.[9] Clearly, the introduction of such radical new policies as the building of Hadrian's and the Antonine Walls in the second century must have carried serious implications for the garrison-pattern at the time elsewhere in the North West.[10] We are confined therefore to basic observations: for example, it is reasonably clear that the Agricolan dispositions were thin on the ground, but that they were heavily supplemented during the forty years which separated Agricola's departure and the building of Hadrian's Wall, during which time the consolidation of the Lake District was undertaken. We may further assume that during the second century the emphasis moved northwards to the frontier and its immediate hinterland. The third century, following Severus' and Caracalla's military and diplomatic initiatives in Scotland, saw more settled conditions and apparently the withdrawal of some garrisons. The fourth century witnessed a renewed build-up with every indication of a strong garrison in the second half of the century.

This picture, whilst obviously unsatisfactory, may be supplemented in other ways: fort sizes (particularly where they change at a particular site) may help us at least to identify the type of unit likely to have been in garrison.[11] The average size may be put at three to four acres, and normally holding a *Cohors Quingenaria Peditata*; there is, however, a significant group of smaller forts, in which those close to three acres presumably held a similar type of cohort, whilst the very small ones (for example, Ambleside at 1·9 acres and Castleshaw II at 0·65 acres) probably held detachments of units. Above the average (up to six or seven acres) was a group which will largely have held *Cohortes Equitatae* or *Alae*.

The army was, however, far more than simply an occupying force to ensure subjection; economically, it provided markets to be supplied by imported and locally-produced goods. As such, it acted as a stimulus to the organisation and efficiency of local farmers and craftsmen. No less potent will have been its social and cultural influence; until the time of the emperor Septimius Severus, serving soldiers were not permitted to marry. This, however, did not prevent a substantial part of the *vici* outside the forts being occupied by the 'friends' of soldiers. Subsequent to Severus' army reforms, 'married quarters' will have fulfilled the same role. A further social effect of the Roman Army will have derived from the fact that presumably many of the soldiers will have turned to farming in the North West (see further below).

Culturally, the army's effects were diverse: we may assume that it will have been a stimulus to the use of Latin, at least as a medium for trade. As we shall see later, its effect upon such important elements of life as religion and leisure-time, will have been considerable also. We should probably not make the mistake of underestimating the degree of Romanisation probably achieved in the flourishing *vici* of the North West.

The military occupation of course did have a primary objective, namely, the pacification and 'Romanisation' of the area. Empire-wide it was a predictable policy that a state with only limited resources in military manpower would attempt to secure the co-operation rather than the costly hostility of subject-peoples. It is uncertain whether this objective was ever totally achieved: as we have seen, the second century was a disturbed period in the north: and it is doubtful whether Roman troops could ever afford to turn their backs totally with impunity.[12] In microcosm the tombstone of Flavius Romanus from Ambleside[13] spells out the danger: for with unusual frankness, he is described as having been killed by the enemy *inside* his fort. Further, we may begin to wonder whether Roman buildings, which are described as having 'collapsed through old age',[14] may in fact have met a more violent end.

42

As we saw, the immediate pre-Roman history of the Brigantes shows them used as a 'client-kingdom' by Rome, and balanced between the pro-Roman sentiments of Cartimandua and the hostility of Venutius, her consort. A political map of the Brigantes at this stage would, however, be hard to draw: there is no real indication of the chief centres of Cartimandua and Venutius, and many of the hill-forts lack anything approaching a detailed chronology. It has, however, been surmised that Cartimandua's main strength was the fertile agricultural land to the east of the Pennines, whilst Venutius, the warlord patron of horse-breeders and metal-workers, was strong in the west.

What degree of Romanisation, then, was achieved amongst the Brigantes? It has often been said that Romanisation meant urbanisation: politically, socially and economically, the Roman Empire was organised around towns. In the south of Britain, a deliberate policy of urbanisation was pursued from an early stage, built around the willingness of tribal leaders to undertake a considerable element of local government responsibility.

Whilst for the Brigantes military activity can never have been far away, major towns did develop: early in the third century the *canabae* outside the legionary fortress at York achieved the elevated status of *Colonia*. Aldborough (Isurium) became the centre of Brigantian local government, which obviously demonstrates that, as in the south, amongst the Brigantes too the Romans could rely on a Romanised hierarchy to shoulder the main facets of a civilian administration. To a degree, the existence of a Romanised tutelary deity—the Birrens *Brigantia*—confirms this. The Brigantes of course occupied a large area: it seems that sub-groups existed within it: for example, Ptolemy's *Portus Setantiorum*, sited apparently at the mouth of the Wyre, suggests the existence in Lancashire of a group called the *Setantii*, although no inscription has been found to confirm this or to give a clue to its precise location.

More certain is the sub-group (*civitas*) of the Carvetii, whose centre was presumably Carlisle; the general location of this *civitas* is confirmed by two inscriptions—from Old Penrith[15] and from Brougham.[16] The administrative *territorium* of the *civitas* cannot be described with any certainty, although it is a plausible suggestion[17] that the Middleton milestone, which records a distance of fifty-three Roman miles, presumably from Carlisle, may mark its boundary at this point.

The excavation programme in Carlisle, though still in its early days, has begun to reveal buildings whose scope is consistent with a local government role—for example, the large hypocausted house at Keays Lane[18] and the suggested *Praetorium*, classical temple and *mansio* elsewhere in the Lanes area. Carlisle seems therefore to have buildings well in advance of any other urban site in the North West, and it may be this that evinced the 'civic pride' evident in the discovery of mural-crowned figures. These buildings appear to have flourished between the mid-second and mid-fourth centuries,[19] before which time we may assume that Carlisle was a growing town (*vicus*) outside the fort: the long-lived house on Blackfriars Street may be seen as a part of this.[20]

Whilst lacking the status of Carlisle, the other towns in the North West which grew up outside the forts (*vici*) will have lacked nothing in vitality. The life of the *vici*

Plate 19   Dea Brigantia: the goddess Brigantia, the tutelary deity of the Brigantes, represented as a 'Winged Victory' (from Birrens in Dumfriesshire; now in The National Museum of Antiquities, Edinburgh)

Plate 20   Vindolanda: the fort and *vicus*

is known only in fragments; only the site at Vindolanda has seen large-scale excavation, and the only other sizeable *vicus* excavation has been the series of campaigns in the Deansgate area of Manchester. The dangers of generalising from a few examples cannot be overstressed. The sizes of these settlements can only be guessed at, since none has come anywhere near to being totally examined, although aerial photography in a few cases suggests a considerable size (e.g. Piercebridge in Co. Durham and Old Carlisle).

It is unlikely that these were towns planned, like the *civitas* centres, outwards from a central market square, but rather were ribbon developments that grew along one or more of the fort's access roads: at Watercrook, for example, excavation has revealed substantial *vicus* areas on the south-east and north-east sides of the fort. We may assume that they grew into whatever shape and size that local conditions suggested. One factor that has emerged from the limited excavations of such sites is that we should not generalise about their chronologies: it is over-simple to say that their life-spans and fluctuations correspond with those of their fort, because that clearly is not the case. It does appear, however, that they did in the majority of known cases become established very rapidly in the wake of fort development, as at Watercrook.[21] There is certainly a considerable number which do not appear to have lasted beyond the late second or early third centuries (e.g. Watercrook, Manchester, Lancaster, Ribchester), whilst others run later (e.g. Old Carlisle, and Old Penrith). Ribchester is in fact rather a curious case, for although finds suggest an absence of *vicus* activity beyond the early third century, there are two mid-third century

45

building inscriptions which must refer to extra-mural buildings. Ribchester has one further curiosity: its name is given in the *Ravenna Cosmography* as *Bresnetenaci Veteranorum*, which as Richmond[22] pointed out, surely suggests local settlement of discharged soldiers. Excavations in 1980 on the north side of the fort did produce evidence of an Antonine rampart and ditch, which might indicate that the *vicus* was defended, and so provide tangible evidence of a 'special status'.

Activities within a *vicus* were obviously varied, but broadly must have centred around the provision of the services that a fort's soldiers would require, or upon which they could be persuaded to spend money. Major buildings will have included bath-houses, temples, a *mansio*: but the majority of buildings will have been of the 'strip-house' type—long rectangular buildings with their gable-ends facing on to the street. Many of these will have been transversely partitioned, with the front section providing a shop, and living accommodation behind it. At the back, there was often a yard, which may have acted as a place of manufacture for whatever was sold in the front. It is likely that many of the native craftsmen, particularly metal-workers, found the economic context of *vicus* an attraction, for it provided them with a ready market. Whilst a good deal of this was probably run on a private and individual basis, at Manchester there seemed to be a larger organisation involved; for beside the road leading out of the fort's north gate there was a large collection of iron-furnaces with evidence of sheds and 'lean-to' buildings. It is likely that the *vici* will have provided contexts for a wide variety of industry—pottery, metal-work, medications, leather goods, and so on. We do not of course have sufficient evidence to determine the origins of population in the *vici*, though it may be assumed that whilst some came from diverse parts of Britain, many will have been local craftsmen who welcomed the opportunity provided by the organisation of the *vicus* and the market thus made available. Another substantial element in the population will have been provided by the 'unofficial' families of serving soldiers. Although not permitted until the time of Septimius Severus' army reforms to contract legal marriages whilst on service, many did have unofficial 'wives' whose status was recognised when the soldier was discharged.

Inns and bars must have been common buildings in the *vici*, and most will probably have had a hotel or posting-house (*mansio*): the *mansio* at Vindolanda has been completely excavated, and is seen to have had a series of rooms arranged around an open courtyard, with a small bath-house. Such a building will have been used principally by official travellers, particularly the couriers of the imperial post.

The bath-house was an inevitable building, and will have been used by both soldiers and civilians. Most of the *vicus* bath-houses were uncomplicated in plan, conforming either to a linear arrangement of rooms (as at Hardknott, which was incidentally one fort in North-West England that did not have a *vicus*) or to an arrangement of rooms alongside a courtyard or open exercise area (*palaestra*): the latter in effect was a scaled-down version of the major bath-houses found in Italy. The fuel which will have been required for a bath-house will over a protracted period have resulted in a large-scale cutting of timber, which in its turn undoubtedly helped to change many aspects of the local environment over the centuries.

Plate 21   Vindolanda: the *mansio*

Whilst not perhaps 'religious' in the way that a Christian would interpret that word, the Roman or Romanised Briton will have erected many shrines to his various gods. Few of such religious buildings are known in the *vici* from surviving structures, although the shrine of Mithras at Carrawburgh on Hadrian's Wall is a notable exception. Most of such buildings are known from characteristic artefacts, fragments of statuary and from inscriptions. Mithraism had its chief currency amongst soldiers, and evidence has come from Housesteads, Castlesteads, Manchester and Chester. In addition, the headless statue of a Mithraic figure (probably 'vandalised' by early Christians) has come from the vicinity of Wigan—serving to keep alive the long debate on the likely Roman origins of that town.

It is clear from the surviving evidence that a rich variety of cults existed: Roman cults will have included the Olympian deities as well as the obligatory cult of the Emperors. Besides these the army and merchants will have brought with them cults from further afield, such as Mithraism itself and the Egyptian cults of Isis and Serapis. The majority of religious centres, however, will have belonged to deities which represented a synthesis of Roman and native cults—such as Mars Cocidius at Bewcastle, or Apollo Maponus at Ribchester. These synthesised deities must have been an effective feature of Romanisation, providing Roman and native with a shared religious interest. Few, if any, of the temples will have been of the classical type, but will have been derivatives of the multi-shaped Romano-Celtic type, as has been recognised as having formalised in the Roman period the worship of the local 'water-nymph' Coventina, at Carrawburgh.

Plate 22   Carlisle: religious dedication to the 'synthesised' deity Mars Ocelus, coupled with a dedication to the imperial cult: 'to Mars Ocelus and to the godhead of the emperor . . .' The emperor's name has been erased following his death

Plate 23   Lancaster: dedication to Mars, made by a unit of Bargemen and their commander. It reads: 'To the god Mars, Sabinus the Commander and the soldiers of the unit of Bargemen make their vow'

Eventually, the tide of Christianity will have found its way into the *vici*. No Christian church has as yet been recognised in the North West: rather, Christians are recognisable from personal items (jewellery, lamps and so on) and from graffiti, such as Chi Rho and Alpha-Omega devices. It is also likely that tombstones, which describe the deceased person's age as a particular figure 'more or less', have a Christian significance. Stones of this sort have been recognised at both Brougham and Carlisle.[23] The earliest known Christian find from a North-West site comes from Manchester in the form of a piece of *amphora* bearing a graffito of the well-known word-square which makes up the words *Pater Noster*, or *Our Father* [24]

Plate 24   Carlisle: tombstone of Flavius Antigonus Papias. It reads: 'Sacred to the gods of the Under-world, Flavius Antigonus Papias, a Greek citizen, lived for sixty years more or less . . .'

The organisation of the *vici* is more open to doubt:[25] clearly the use of the word *vicani* (townspeople) implies some kind of organisation.[26] Further, the abbreviation *Vik. Mag.*[27] has sometimes been thought to stand for 'Vikanorum Magistri' (Elders) though it might more likely be that *Mag* conceals the name of Old Carlisle, making the inscription parallel to the Vindolanda example.[28] It is likely, however, that final jurisdiction in the affairs of the *vicani* lay in the hands of the fort commander—or perhaps shared with the nearest civilian authority;[29] at Vindolanda, for example, it must surely have been a military decision that caused the fort and *vicus* to exchange sites. Lancaster may provide a parallel case in that a bath-house, which may have been part of a *mansio*, was obliterated by the defences of the fourth-century fort.[30] That the people of the *vici* were, however, capable of organisation is supported by the evidence of their literacy—in the form of inscriptions, graffiti and above all writing-tablets.

Plate 25   Chester: the amphitheatre

Plate 26   Bowness-on-Solway: fine and coarse wares of mid-second century date

50

A further aspect of Romanised town-life is entertainment and ceremonial. The legionary fortress at Chester had a stone-built amphitheatre close at hand;[31] and the discovery of a pottery face-mask at Wilderspool[32] may provide a pointer to the type of entertainment available. Whether similar, though smaller, sites existed in the *vici* of auxiliary forts is not clear.

A striking indication of the resilience of the *vicus*-type of development is gained not just from their size, but also from the remote and inhospitable conditions in which they developed. For, although it appears that Hardknott did not support a *vicus*, platforms cut in the hillside on the south side of Maiden Castle-on-Stainmore were clearly intended to support rectangular buildings such as one would expect in a *vicus*.

The *vicus*, then, provided an incentive for craftsmen to come and set up business: they may even have been officially encouraged to bring themselves within the organised scope of these sites. The *vici* were not, however, the only sources of manufactured goods available to the North-West's population. Besides the influx of goods from other parts of Britain and even the Continent, we have evidence of local industrial sites, some of which were undoubtedly directly controlled by the army.

The most completely known of the military depots in the North West is the one at Holt in Denbighshire, which serviced the legionary fortress at Chester.[33] The depot was producing tiles and pottery from the late first century into the third, with the peak of activity in the first half of the second. The twenty-acre site produced evidence

Plate 27   Walton-le-Dale: foundation trenches of timber shed in the 'depot'

of 'barracks', a building interpreted as an officer's house, and a bath-house—in addition to the industrial buildings themselves. It is similarly possible that the impressive buildings located at Walton-le-Dale, a site which contains hearths and wells, should also be interpreted as belonging to a legionary depot; the date-range of these, too, appears to be late first to early third century.[34]

Besides these major military depots, smaller (presumably auxiliary) depots have been located: Muncaster presumably supplied Ravenglass and Hardknott,[35] Scalesceugh perhaps Carlisle and Old Penrith; in addition a large tilery was discovered at Brampton;[36] both of these were operating in the early second century, and should perhaps be connected with the development of the Stanegate *limes*. The Brampton works, which saw the largest examination of all such sites in the North West, was observed to be of markedly inferior construction compared to the legionary equivalent at Holt. It is thought that in the case of Brampton, the depot was sufficiently close to Old Church fort for the living accommodation to have been provided there. Two further sites of this type, approximately a mile apart, but on the same contour, have been located at Quernmore, some three miles east of Lancaster;[37] at one a crudely constructed tile kiln and a better pottery kiln, together with evidence for iron-working, were located, and thought to fall within the date-range of *c*. A.D. 80–160. No evidence of accommodation or administrative buildings was recovered.

Plate 28   Quernmore: a pottery kiln

Excavations at both Quernmore and Lancaster have put the connection of the two sites beyond question: die-linked stamps of the *Ala Sebosiana* have been recovered at both, and analysis of the clays has confirmed the connection. It should, however, be noted that fragments of hollow voussoir tiles[38] recovered from the sub-floor debris of the third-century bath-house were found to bear no relationship to the Quernmore material. Since these must post-date the mid-third century rebuilding (RIB 605), it confirms the impression that the local tilery was no longer in operation and that supplies must by that time have been organised on a different basis.

The close approximation of dates from sites of this nature suggests that their phasing-out was an act of policy, and presumably reflects two things: first the main phases of building of military sites were complete and repair work would (hopefully) not require building-materials on such a scale. Second, larger mass-producing sites elsewhere in the country were presumably by that time (i.e. late second/early third centuries) well able to cope with the demands made of them. This is obviously true of pottery, where the bulk of the military market in the later second century was being serviced by east Gaulish Samian, black-burnished products from Dorset, and Nene Valley ware.

Industrial activity, mainly iron- and salt-working, has been noted at a number of Cheshire sites: extensive evidence for metal-working, together with a widespread area of sheds and workshops has been revealed at Heronbridge,[39] ranged on both sides of Watling Street and close by the Dee, a little south of Chester. Activity seems to have continued here from the late first into the third century, although it is not clear whether the site was 'private' or run upon military lines. A similar doubt hangs over Northwich, Middlewich and Whitchurch, all of which have yielded abundant evidence of industrial activity. Conceivably this originated in the context of a *vicus*, since all three sites had military phases. It may well be, however, that when military occupation came to an end, the industrial activity, presumably in the hands of civilians, was able to continue.[40]

Finally, at the point where the road from Northwich to Walton-le-Dale crosses the Mersey, is situated the most extensive of the North-West's industrial sites—at Wilderspool and Stockton Heath. The site, which apparently, as at Heronbridge, straddles the road, has seen a number of extensive excavations,[41] the largest being at the turn of the century. Many different industrial activities have been recognised—working in iron, bronze and lead, pottery, tile- and glass-making, as well as enamelling.[42]

The site is criss-crossed with fence-posts and ditches, which are presumably property demarcations, though the latter could conceivably be water-channels. A few stone buildings have been located, but the majority are of timber construction; whilst most are basically rectilinear, a circular one located in the excavations of 1976 gives rise to speculation about the nature of the inhabitants. Such a building strongly suggests a native British origin, and it has been suggested that the 'trade-mark' type of mortarium stamp might in fact simply represent illiterate blundering, rather as occurs on copies of Roman third-century radiate coins.

The products of the Wilderspool pottery-kilns have been traced in many parts of

53

Plate 29   Wilderspool: rows of posts and trenches (property divisions), and the remains of a circular hut (on the top left)

the North West, and as far north as the Antonine Wall. Although a putative set of 'defences' has often been assumed to represent the remains of an Agricolan fort, the dating evidence so far recovered is in fact consistent with initial occupation at the end of the first century and carried on into the third. It would seem that the high-point of activity falls in that period, though a scatter of later material[43] indicates that occupation of some kind continued into the fourth century.

The nature of sites like Wilderspool, Heronbridge and the industrial areas of the *vici* suggests that the workers were principally native craftsmen who for one reason or another (voluntarily or under persuasion) came into the organised areas to work—perhaps to secure a better hold on the assured markets which the Roman occupation offered.

The bulk of the population, we can assume, remained as they had long been— arable farmers and pastoralists. However, the most obvious difference in the rural landscape between the North West and the rest of the province was the former's lack of what is generally, though perhaps misleadingly, regarded as typical of the Romanised countryside—the villa. The villa estate required land and finance;[44] as such it would have been beyond the aspiration of ordinary farmers, *vicus*-dwellers and auxiliary veterans. Legionary veterans, too, though better rewarded than their auxiliary colleagues, would probably not have been able to finance such a venture. Evidently, local government did not, west of the Pennines at least, produce the

54

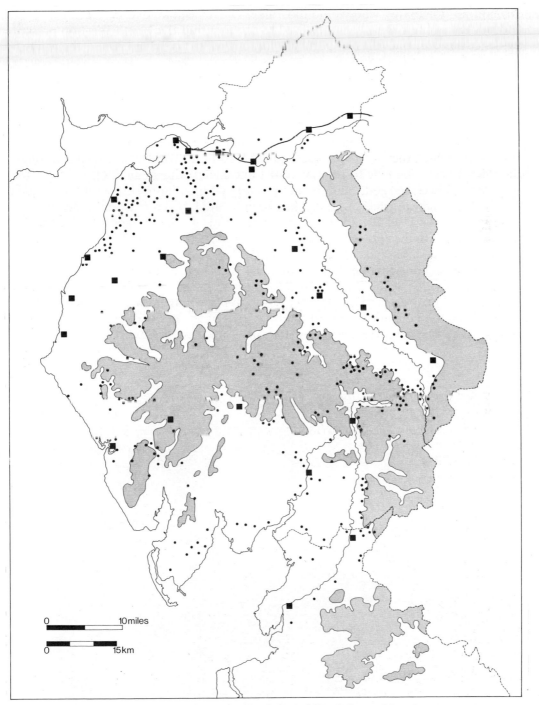

Fig. 3   Rural sites in Cumbria and North Lancashire

55

Brigantian 'magnates' who would most likely have been able to invest in this way. Indeed, the point is sharply emphasised by the fact that the North West on present evidence has only one villa comparable with those of the Lowland zone—the winged-corridor house at Kirk Sink.[45]

However, whilst the North West lacks villas in its rural economy, it is likely that of the many rural sites now recorded some at least will have belonged to Roman military veterans. Although there is at present no evidence to confirm Richmond's hypothesis concerning large-scale veteran settlement in the Fylde area of Lancashire, we may be confident that some discharged soldiers will have stayed in retirement in the area in which they served. Evidence may exist in the form of a dedication found at Foley Farm, one mile to the north of Lancaster;[46] this dedication made to the local (possibly river-) god, Jalonus, was put up by Julius Januarius, a retired cavalry NCO. Although no trace of a farm has been located, it is a reasonable hypothesis that Januarius served at Lancaster and received his discharge land payment in the close vicinity of the fort. We might further expect that areas devoted to such a purpose might show signs of centuriation.[47]

Although a considerable number of rural sites—particularly in the area of the upper Lune Valley—have been known for a long time,[48] it would be true to say that in general, until recent years at least, less attention has been paid to this aspect of the Roman occupation than to the problems of the military dispositions themselves. Recently, however, aerial research programmes[49] followed up by fieldwork

Plate 30   Watercrook: an enamelled silver brooch

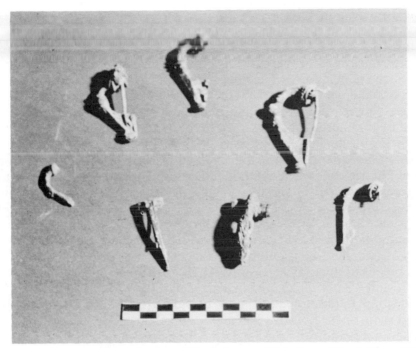

Plate 31   Watercrook: a selection of 'cloak fasteners' (photograph by J. Thompson)

Plate 32   Watercrook: iron finger-ring with onyx setting depicting Achilles (photograph by J. Thompson)

57

and limited excavation, have begun to throw more light on to the picture of rural settlement.

Two factors have been amply demonstrated: first, we clearly have to reject the notion, often advanced in the past, that apart from the areas of the Roman sites themselves, the population of the North West was thin.[50] Secondly, it is clear from the locations of agricultural sites that there must have been a strong economic interdependence between the Roman and native populations, a point also effectively confirmed by the 'stores-lists' preserved in the Vindolanda tablets.[51]

The plotting of sites has proceeded much further in Cumbria than in Lancashire; conditions in the latter do not readily lend themselves to aerial research; thus the number of known sites is small, although finds of Roman material suggest that the Roman roads and the river valleys will have provided the chief foci for settlement. Nonetheless, possible traces of the Romano-British landscape have been observed on the eastern flank of the West Lancashire mosses; and there are signs that the higher ground in the Fylde may have supported settlement.[52]

North of Lancashire, considerable settlement has been observed on the limestone of the Ribblehead area, as at Gauber High Pasture and Colt Park.[53] In North Lancashire and Cumbria, the principal areas of settlement are located in the valley floors and slopes of the communications corridors provided by the Lune and Eden rivers, and again on the Solway Plain and the northern slopes of the Lake District.[54]

Although excavation of rural sites has been very limited, it would appear a

Plate 33   Colt Park, Ribblesdale: a circular hut (with the entrance on the right) and field boundaries

reasonable assumption that a high proportion of them, even if multi-period, was active in the Roman period. It is similarly reasonable to suppose that many, if not most of the sites, both arable and pastoral, enjoyed an 'economic relationship' with the Roman forts and *vici*. In other words, they were producing grain surplus to their taxation requirement, and their animal husbandry was to an extent organised to take account of the Roman market for meat.[55]

A total picture is of course beyond recovery; particularly in the valley floors and on the lower slopes subsequent agricultural activity has destroyed a good deal of the evidence. However, the density of sites located, particularly on the good land of the valley floors, suggests a picture of intense agricultural activity, based upon a mixed arable/pastoral economy. Evidence accumulated from the Eller Beck sites in the Lune Valley[56] suggests an extensive system of 'celtic' fields, spreading up the valley slopes and perhaps centred on the valley floor. The presence of 'mixed-farming' sites on the fells (for example, Waitby, Crosby Ravensworth and Crosby Garrett) perhaps indicates an attempt to utilise the slopes in a manner similar to that of the valleys themselves with cultivation carried probably to a higher altitude than nowadays.[57] On the whole, however, the higher-level sites (that is, above approximately 800 feet) carry, in the evidence of dykes and large 'fields', the indications of stock-management and pastoralism.[58] In the case of Eller Beck and Waitby, it has been shown that in the later Roman period there is evidence of arable land giving way to a pastoral use.[59] Obviously, life will have been harder at the higher levels, and there is no evidence of permanent settlement higher than 900–1,000 feet.

Sites are variable in shape and size, though in general they conform to the pattern of single farmsteads rather than groups which might merit being described as 'villages'.[60] They are generally enclosed or 'defended' in such a way as to keep out casual marauders—whether animal or human. In shape they are generally sub-rectangular (such as Cantsfield at the confluence of the Greta and the Lune), or circular (as at Wolsty Hall on the Solway Plain)[61] and have single entrances.

Internal buildings are circular or rectangular huts with, as one would expect, considerable variation in size.[62] The distinction between the two has to be treated carefully, as it may reflect change over a long period, as at Gauber High Pasture[63] where excavation showed rectangular buildings to be of ninth-century date. For obvious reasons, the distinction in shape was first observed in stone-built (that is, higher level) sites, and was thought to reflect tribal differences.[64] Since, however, some lowland sites have now also exhibited a change from circular to rectangular (for example, at Wolsty Hall and Cross Hill, Penrith)[65] the distinction is much more likely to reflect a developmental (chronological) sequence. Indeed, we might see circular buildings associated with Roman pottery of second-century date, and rectangular ones with pottery of third- and fourth-century dates.[66] It should, however, be noted that not all sites show this development, and recent excavations at Fingland[67] showed clear evidence of a circular hut associated with late Roman pottery. Whilst the huts may be placed anywhere within the enclosures, a striking phenomenon is found at Castle Folds on Orton Scar[68] where a defensive stone wall circuit has circular and rectilinear buildings constructed against its interior face. Building

Plate 34   Cantsfield: a sub-rectangular farm enclosure

materials vary; in general, stone is used where it is readily available particularly at the higher levels (for example, at Maiden Castle-on-Stainmore). Elsewhere timber or wattle was used under a thatched roof, as at Wolsty Hall, whilst the Fingland round-hut[69] was apparently built of turfs on a stone foundation.

The relationship of agricultural sites to Roman roads, forts and *vici* needs no emphasis; the sites of native (and perhaps veteran) farmers were linked by trackways into the Roman network, and their position was clearly to a degree dictated by the 'Roman topography' of the area. In all, we can see a period in which relatively intense land-use developed to satisfy the larger markets created by the soldiers and dependents of the occupying army.[70]

Clearly there is much research to be done, particularly on the detailed nature of the economic basis of the sites. Whilst aerial survey and field-work will continue to advance the picture, the excavation of more sites is clearly required. It is however possible with the present state of the evidence to see in part the relationship between the Roman troops and the native population—whether as craftsmen or farmers. To a degree, all were harmonised into a Romano-British economy; the native population was producing goods, manufactured or agricultural, on a commercial as well as a taxation basis, for this will explain the presence of items like Samian pottery on native sites, which must have been acquired in return for goods.

In short, therefore, it would appear to be far from the truth to argue for a 'conquerors and vanquished' type of relationship in the North West. The Romans were a stimulus; within limits the local population became Romanised. Whilst progress was less marked and dramatic than in Lowland Britain, it would still be reasonable to assert that Roman and native lived together to mutual advantage.

60

Notes

(N.B. References to modern books and articles are given in an abbreviated form; these references are itemised in full in the Bibliography.)

1. e.g. Davies (1977).
2. Potter (1979), 315 ff.
3. Rivet (1970).
4. Ward (1973); Hassall (1976).
5. Richmond and Crawford (1949).
6. e.g. Richardson and Richardson (1980).
7. e.g. in Potter (1979), 317.
8. Hassall (1976); cf. Richmond (1935) and Heurgon (1951).
9. Potter (1979), 337.
10. Hartley (1980), 5 f.
11. Potter (1979), 146 f.
12. Hartley (1980), 5 f.
13. *JRS* 53 (1963), 160.
14. e.g. the bath-house and Basilica at Lancaster (*RIB* 605) which were rebuilt in the 260s.
15. *RIB* 933.
16. *JRS* 55 (1965), 224; the inscription is of mid-third century date.
17. Birley, E. B. (1953); Potter (1979), 195; the milestone is recorded as *RIB* 2283; the possibility of other *Civitates* is explored by Jones, R. F. J. (1981), who mentions Kirkby Thore as a possible centre.
18. *Britannia* XII (1981), 325 f.
19. *Britannia* XIII (1982), 343 f.
20. *Britannia* IX (1978), 423.
21. Potter (1979), 187.
22. Richmond (1945).
23. *RIB* 787 (Brougham); *RIB* 955 (Carlisle).
24. *Britannia* X (1979), 353.
25. Salway (1980); Jones, R. F. J. (1981).
26. e.g. *RIB* 1700 from Vindolanda.
27. on *RIB* 899 from Old Carlisle.
28. Hassall (1976)
29. Salway (1980), basing his suggestion on the Roman jurist, Ulpian (*Digest* 50, 1, 30).
30. *Britannia* V (1974), 418.
31. Thompson (1976).
32. Thompson (1965), 84.
33. Grimes (1930); Thompson (1965), 53 ff.
34. *Britannia* XIII (1982), 352.
35. Bellhouse (1960b).
36. Hogg (1965).
37. *Britannia* III (1972), 313; *Britannia* IV (1973), 283.
38. Shotter (1983).
39. Thompson (1965), 60 ff.
40. Jones (1974), 147 f.
41. Thompson (1965), 67 ff.
42. Tylcote (1962), 222 ff.
43. Webster (1975).
44. Branigan (1980).
45. near Gargrave; see *Britannia* V (1974), 416 and *Britannia* VI (1975), 238.
46. *RIB* 600.
47. e.g. Richardson, A. (1982), for an area near Old Penrith.
48. R.C.H.M. (1936); Collingwood, W. G. (1908 and 1909).
49. e.g. Higham and Jones (1975).
50. See now the distribution map in Higham (1980), 42.
51. Bowman and Thomas, (1983).
52. Jones (1979), 79 ff.
53. *YAJ* 41 (1966), 559–60; King (1978).
54. Higham and Jones (1975); Higham (1978, 1979, 1980, 1982).

55. Jones (1975); Bowman and Thomas (1983); Davies (1971); Manning (1975).
56. Lowndes (1963 and 1964); Higham (1979).
57. Pennington (1970).
58. e.g. Aughertree Fell (Bellhouse, 1967).
59. Higham and Jones (1975), 40 ff; Higham (1979), 34.
60. Higham (1980), 41.
61. Blake (1959), 7 ff.
62. Higham (1979).
63. King (1978).
64. Collingwood, W.G. (1909).
65. *Britannia* VIII (1977), 377.
66. Blake (1959), 7 ff.
67. Richardson (1977).
68. Richmond (1933); Higham (1979).
69. Richardson (1977), 57.
70. Manning (1975).

6

The Last Years

We have seen that Severus by armed force and then his son Caracalla by diplomacy appear to have secured with the Scottish tribes some kind of agreement which apparently brought a large measure of peace to the north for a good deal of the third century. It is less clear, however, how far the military grip was relaxed: a major problem in the approach to this question lies in the nature of the evidence: in general, the pottery is less clearly dated for the third and fourth centuries than it is for the first and second. Further, coin-loss evidence is also less reliable for the period, being complicated by the monetary crises that deepened as the century wore on, and by the *annona militaris*—the practice of paying troops at least partly in kind, which started late in the century.

It is certain that (with the exception of the forts) the Cumberland coast defences, which had been abandoned late in the second century, were not in use during the third—although, as we shall see, there *is* evidence which suggests a selective reactivation in the fourth. Building-inscriptions and other evidence of building activity indicate that forts were certainly being kept in repair in the first half of the third century (for example, at Ribchester, Manchester, Lancaster, Watercrook, Old Carlisle, Old Penrith).[1] The second half of the century, however, presents a more confused picture.

In the first place, the civilian authority that was in being by the 260s in the form of the *Civitas Carvetiorum* implies internal peace in the North West and perhaps a desire to place more of the burden of administration on to the local population. It is likely, too, that Hadrian's Wall was left unmolested during this period: the result was probably that garrisons were reduced or even removed, as certainly happened at Watercrook, where a fresh coin of A.D. 320 in the top of the ditch-fill implies demilitarisation by that stage. There is evidence to suggest that some Hadrian's Wall forts (for example, Castlesteads, Birdoswald, Halton Chesters, Rudchester and Wallsend) and the Wall itself fell into a state of considerable disrepair. It is possible that these sites were not actually abandoned, but held by token numbers: it has been suggested that the new, smaller type of barrack-block shown to have been built at Housesteads and other Wall forts in the early fourth century implies a reduced and perhaps less well organised garrison.

Secondly, changes in the nature of the army command structure, where unit commanders were much more likely to have been soldiers risen from the ranks than the men of higher social status that had been usual before, may have meant a loss of discipline. Further, fewer of the troops were now formed into regular auxiliary units, and more reliance was placed on the units of irregulars. Internally, therefore, peaceful conditions together with the contemporary state of the army itself seem to have combined to produce a relaxed, if not lax, holding of the North West in the later third century.

If the province was not troubled with anxieties on its northern frontier, there were certainly problems elsewhere, which will have had their effect in the north. Inflation ran wild in the middle of the third century—at least partly due to the fact that successive emperors in their efforts to maintain their positions 'printed money' in order to hand out funds they did not possess. The resultant chaos is evidenced by the large number of often very poor standard 'radiate copies' in circulation; there were clearly a number of copying centres for these in the north including (probably) Brougham and Carlisle. Further, attempts made by emperors between c. A.D. 270–300 to remove this 'bad money' seem in the case of Britain to have largely failed. The demoralising effect of economic chaos can be paralleled from more recent history.

Again, Severus' reforms of the army and its command structure, which led to promotion through the ranks to senior army command—and higher—had the effect by the middle of the century of making anarchy virtually endemic in the Empire. It led not only to a constant stream of 'pretenders', but eventually to breakaway movements such as the Independent Empire of the Gauls (*Imperium Galliarum*) in which between A.D. 259 and 273 the Germanies, Gaul and Britain completely severed their connection with the central government and its officials. How far (if at all) this led to the removal of troops from Britain is unclear. The British army's loyalty to the new rulers is evidenced by such inscriptions as the Lancaster Bathhouse stone,[2] from which the name of Postumus, the creator of the *Imperium Galliarum*, was subsequently removed.

Although this rebellion collapsed in A.D. 273, to be followed by a series of rather stronger central government emperors, the eventual 'solution', enacted by Diocletian, was the establishment of first a dyarchy, and a little later, a tetrarchy. However, in Britain, Carausius, who had been appointed by Maximian (Diocletian's fellow-*Augustus*), to keep the English Channel and the North Sea free of pirates, decided that the principle of split power could be extended: he issued a coin with three obverse heads (his own, Diocletian's and Maximian's) with the legend CARAVSIVS ET FRATRES SVI (Carausius and his brothers). Since Diocletian and Maximian failed to regard Carausius as their brother, his position in A.D. 287 became *ipso facto* rebellious. Carausius maintained himself until A.D. 293, when he was murdered by his associate, Allectus, who survived until ousted three years later by the central government in the person of Constantius Chlorus.

The details of the rebellion do not concern us except in so far as it was a period when attention was paid to the problems of coastal defence. Although not of uniform date, the Saxon-Shore fort system owed a good deal of its impetus to this period, and Allectus' 'Galley' coin-reverses stress a similar preoccupation. The new forts were architecturally very different from their predecessors, particularly with their artillery bastions, and indicate a transition in Roman tactical thinking from the 'police-station' to the 'defended strong-point'.

The effect of Allectus' attempts to hold his rebel island against the tetrarchs has long been thought to have been a denuding of northern garrisons, leading to an attack on the frontier from the north. There is evidence for both delapidation and demolition in the north in the late third century, and for fire damage at Ravenglass.

An inscription records Constantius' involvement in rebuilding at Birdoswald, and other Hadrian's Wall and hinterland forts certainly saw reconstruction in the early fourth century.[3] But no evidence points unequivocally to *enemy* attack at that time.

Constantius was in Britain on at least two occasions—in 296 to crush the rebellion of Carausius and Allectus, and again campaigning in the north in 305–6 against the Picts, and it may well have been in the course of this second visit that he set in train the rebuilding programme of forts in the north—not only on Hadrian's Wall, but also at sites like Bainbridge and other Pennine forts. Recent work at Housesteads has demonstrated that the third-century barrack-block in the fort's north-east corner had probably decayed, and was replaced early in the fourth century by a far less formal unit consisting of 'chalets' of variable size which were probably stone-built only to half-height. This presumably is to be taken as indicating a different type of usage from that for which the building's predecessor was intended—either a combined military and civilian purpose, or army units of a different type, although this is left in doubt by the *Notitia's* Wall sub-section and difficulties surrounding its date of reference (third or fourth century); the sub-section lists the Wall forts as garrisoned by the same units as are known from third-century inscriptions, which has led to the suggestion[4] that the chronological reference of this section may in fact be third and not fourth century.

It may be that Constantius' view of and presence in Britain brought about a radical 're-think' of tactics to face the new enemy—the Picts; the post of *Dux Britanniarum* (the northern military commander) was probably created at this time. Further, the rebuilding noted at hinterland forts may suggest that the notion of 'defence in depth' was coming to supersede the idea of the Wall as a 'curtain-barrier'. Indeed, the Wall itself, as distinct from its forts, may have been less important in the fourth-century arrangements.[5] Thus the post of *Dux Britanniarum* was now added to that of *Comes Litoris Saxonici*, and the pair represent the two fourth-century 'frontier' armies in Britain: these armies were distinct from the 'field army' which the emperors took on campaign with them. In A.D. 315, Constantine took the title of *Britannicus Maximus*; a particular point of reference is not known, though it may have had some relation to the west coast,[6] or possibly to a continued attention to in-depth readiness, for which Constantine was in fact criticised in antiquity.[7] Possibly, we should date the establishment of the west-coast 'Saxon-shore' forts to this period, although reliable dates are not to hand for Cardiff, Caernarvon or Caer Gybi, and the new fort at Lancaster would appear to be a decade or so later than this.

It is difficult to say how far (if at all) a *coherent* west-coast defence system existed. That the Bristol Channel was a significant base at least later in the century seems to be suggested by the *PR REL* (*Praefectus reliquationis classis*) mosaic in the Nodons temple at Lydney. This, together with the forts at Cardiff, Caernarvon and Caer Gybi, stresses the importance and vulnerability of the Welsh coast; it is further likely that a fleet base in the Bristol Channel will have rendered redundant the legionary fortress at Caerleon (which does not appear to have outlasted the third century). The Bristol Channel base will have linked to the still maintained legionary fortress at Chester, on the Dee estuary, and thence to Lancaster on the Lune estuary, where

Plate 35 Caer Gybi, Holyhead: the fourth-century bastioned fort

Plate 36 Lancaster: the Wery Wall (at top right), the core of the corner bastion of the late fort, and the ditch cut through an earlier bath-house

probably about A.D. 330/340 was built on a different alignment from earlier forts an approximately nine acre enclosure with polygonal corner bastions. It may be significant that Cockersands Moss, just south of Lancaster, was the find-spot of two Nodons statuettes,[8] thus providing a possible link with Lydney and the Bristol Channel.

We may assume that in a fast-changing situation, flexibility was a key word: Vegetius describes camouflaged scout-ships (*pictae*) which were used in the fourth century: Lancaster and Morecambe Bay may have seen novel use made of the *Numerus Barcariorum*,[9] whose normal function will have been lighterage.

Arrangements further north on the coast are not easy to describe precisely: the coastal forts of Ravenglass, Moresby, Maryport and Beckfoot were all occupied in the fourth century, although in the cases of Moresby and Beckfoot it is not clear how long that occupation was sustained. Burrow Walls[10] has produced little other than fourth-century pottery, and may well have been a new—or at least very substantially remodelled—fort of the period. There appears also to have been some fourth-century reoccupation of some of the long-abandoned sites of the coastal system; at Cardurnock (MF 5),[11] for example, pottery suggested occupation both before and after A.D. 367, although the absence of such material at Biglands (MF 1) is sufficient to warn us that this was not a full-scale recommissioning.

The context for some of this work may well have been the visit to Britain in the winter of A.D. 342–3 of the emperor, Constans. The mere fact that the visit was made in the winter is sufficient to indicate that it must have been connected with some emergency, and not just routine in nature. It is known that Constans' visit was in part at least concerned with the *areani* or undercover agents; trouble with them certainly implies disturbance on the northern frontier.

The state of Britain at this time clearly should not be divorced from imperial politics: Constantine's death in 337 had left the Roman world divided between his three surviving sons, Constantine II, Constans and Constantius II. Britain had come within the responsibility of Constantine II, but he was killed in Italy in conflict with Constans in 340. Problems arising out of possible troop withdrawals from Britain by Constantine II and out of possible disaffection in Britain following upon Constantine II's death may have left a situation uncertain enough to encourage Britain's enemies to take advantage—which may well have been the situation with which Constans intended to deal.

The death of Constans in 350 at the hands of a group who proclaimed Magnentius as his successor also suggests a continuing disturbance in Britain: for evidence suggests that Magnentius had particular strength in Britain. It is also likely that he again weakened the provinces' military potential by taking troops to Europe to assert his cause. Magnentius' final defeat at the hands of Constantius II in 353 will have brought still further demoralisation to Britain in its wake—first, two further defeats to add to that in which Constantine II had been killed, and second, a witch-hunt in the province following upon Constantius' reassertion of authority.[12]

In 355 Constantius appointed as western 'Caesar' his cousin Julian. Although Julian's period showed in a sense the strength of Britain in that in 359 it was possible to use the province as a supply base for his efforts to re-establish the Rhine frontier, yet less than two years later the continuing insecurity manifested itself in trouble with the Picts and Scotti (from Ireland), which necessitated the posting to Britain of Lupicinus, a very senior officer, with crack units of the field army. The situation remained tense until it came to a head with the 'Barbarian Conspiracy'[13] in 367, in which all of the enemies of Roman Britain appear to have attacked at once. Such an apparently unlikely event as a 'conspiracy' is made perhaps less unlikely when it is realised how deep was the involvement of Romanised 'barbarians' in Roman political and military affairs. It is possible that leaked information about the contemporary difficulties of the emperor Valentinian I was the trigger for this action:[44] the opportunity was evidently enhanced by the treacherous activities of the *areani*[15] who were disbanded in the wake of the catastrophe.

Valentinian's response was to send to Britain, again with a crack field army, Theodosius, the father of the later emperor Theodosius. Ammianus makes it clear that the situation—military, urban and rural—was one of almost total disarray. We should, however, beware of assuming that every *archaeological* sign of trouble relates to this particular year: as we have seen, 367 had been the climax of nearly two-and-a-half decades of uncertainty and raiding. Theodosius' achievement was considerable—restabilisation of the military situation, the rebuilding of forts and towns, and the restoration of rural peace.

That the majority of north-western sites either survived the barbarian attack or were rebuilt and occupied after, is clear from the ubiquity of the calcite-gritted wares that were the characteristic product of the Crambeck potteries of East Yorkshire in the second half of the fourth century. Similarly, the absence of this type of pottery provides a good indicator of forts that were probably not included in the restoration. It would certainly appear that there was no attempt to recover forts to the north of Hadrian's Wall, and doubt hangs over the continued use of some forts to the south of it (for example, Ribchester and Watercrook), though it has to be stressed in the consideration of this question, as with others, that a number of the forts have as yet no evidence upon which a statement about their occupation at this stage could be based.

Forts in the North West which were reconstructed in this period show no sign of the 'Saxon-shore' architecture as had been employed on the new fort at Lancaster earlier in the century: however, the blocking or narrowing of gateways, which has been seen at a number of sites, possibly represents a similar move in the direction of impenetrability which had characterised the Saxon-shore forts. At both Ravenglass and Bowness-on-Solway[16] excavation has shown that a new constructional technique for internal buildings was employed in this final phase. Instead of foundation beams, buildings were apparently supported on a 'frame' of heavily-packed posts.

Reconstruction is everywhere to be seen in the forts of the Wall and its hinterland—and not just in *rebuilding*, but also in new foundations, such as the two fortlets known to have guarded the road south from Carlisle, at Wreay Hall and Barrock Fell.[17] Nothing, however, is as yet known of the internal layout of these sites. The coasts, too, received attention as they had obviously demonstrated their vulnerability.

As noted above, the west coast saw a selective reactivation of parts of the second-century system, and finds of late fourth-century coins in and around Barrow suggest the possibility of a site in that area, too. The east coast was given a new series of strongly-built signal-towers. In all, then, Theodosius' reconstruction work in the north was a strikingly thorough attempt to take account of all of the problems encountered in the 'Barbarian Conspiracy'. It is probable that recognition of Theodosius' work is to be seen in the use of the tile *Valentia* to apply to the whole of Britain, in honour of the ruling house.[18]

Forty years now remained before Honorius' famous rescript, telling the leaders of the Romano-British *civitates* to look to their own defences, formally spelled out the message that there would now be no Roman troops sent to cover emergencies. This period of four decades, however, showed no obvious slackening of the government's readiness to commit itself: for example, in 382 Magnus Maximus was sent to campaign in the north, though he was subsequently to achieve greater fame through his attempt to unit Gaul and Britain in a single command, and presumably to resuscitate the defunct *Imperium Galliarum*. He maintained himself until 388, and appears to have recorded some positive achievements in strengthening the security of the west coast, through the establishment of tribal protectorates.

However, although the sources are by no means unequivocal in interpretation, it would appear that Maximus' removal of troops to Gaul once again created a volatile situation in the north; indeed it is likely that security matters in the north remained uncertain until another major outbreak, probably in 398, which brought the last positive response by Rome to British affairs. Honorius sent over the Vandal general, Stilicho, who appears to have restored order for the moment, but who either took back to Europe with him, or was closely followed by, a legion from northern Britain.[19]

For ten more years—the first decade of the fifth century—contact was maintained, though increasingly tenuously. It would appear that after about 402 no further supplies of money arrived to pay the army (or such as was left of it); further, evidence suggests an increasing independence within Britain. The second half of the decade saw a new series of 'local' emperors elevated by the army, which we may assume to be the army's response to the failing support from Rome. To this may be linked the action in 408 of independently-minded Britons, perhaps influenced by the 'independent' religious views of Pelagius, in expelling Roman officials and organising the defence of Britain themselves. That this, however, was not a universal view may be assumed from the 'approach' which must have preceded Honorius' rescript. This in fact confirmed that the 'independents' had been wise: there was to be no more help from Rome, and Britain's formal place in the Empire had now lapsed. These 'independent' actions, however, should not be taken to indicate a rejection of everything Roman: the rejection was political: the inhabitants of Britain after all, whether supporting or opposing Rome's current position, were *Romano-British*. As many excavations, particularly of the towns, have shown,[20] the people clearly remained for a considerable time, though perhaps in varying degrees, within the Roman cultural orbit.

The physical fate of north-western sites can only be guessed at, particularly since the means of dating in the fifth century are far from perfect: repairing of chronologically-late vessels, worn late fourth-century coin issues and finds of such vessels as African red-slip ware, all suggest a continued attempt to maintain the familiar way of life. Indeed Christianity, though not always a politically and militarily unifying force, will nonetheless have provided a link with Rome's cultural background. In the North West, as elsewhere, we may reasonably imagine therefore that Roman fortifications continued to provide protection—particularly if we judge from sites like Lancaster, Brough and Brougham, where the medieval castles were erected in some kind of association with the presumably still surviving Roman wall circuit.

The *vici* provide us with a more difficult question: it is unclear how many *vici* still functioned as such in the fourth century: although hypotheses have to be constructed very tentatively because of the very small amount of excavation that has taken place, we can certainly point to some (Manchester, Ribchester, Lancaster, Watercrook and probably also Wilderspool and Walton-le-Dale, for example) where occupation seems not to have extended beyond the third century at the most. At Vindolanda,[21] where the largest area of *vicus* has been recovered, occupation does go into the fourth century, and this is possibly connected with the fact that the *vicani* there appear to have achieved some measure of autonomy.

The question remains, therefore, as to whether in the fourth century the general situation was for military and civilian personnel alike to enjoy the protection afforded by the forts. In this regard, it is worth making the point that, in the face of troop withdrawals during the fourth century, an increasing proportion of the garrisons were probably locally recruited: it will thus have been perfectly natural for them and their families to have regarded themselves as permanently settled in their own particular areas. Short-term, defensibility may have been the chief criterion, though that will not have guaranteed survival long-term; few of the North-West's fort/towns have survived as going concerns even into the middle ages let alone to the present day. Long-term survival required economic strength and links with the outside world. It is not surprising therefore that the North-West's survivors are generally well positioned either on navigable waterways—Chester, Wilderspool/Warrington, Walton-le-Dale/Preston, Manchester, Lancaster, Carlisle, Watercrook/Kendal—or at crucial places on the road system, with the economic and military strength that that gave: hence the defended sites across Stainmore were as important in the middle ages as they had been in the Roman period. In other words, for survival, a site clearly needed to have a significance that transcended its mere place in the Roman defensive network.

In the country, the situation (due to even less excavation than in the towns) is less clear. We may assume that two factors must have been of importance in the late and post-Roman periods: their markets and their ability to continue work unmolested. The degree of fulfilment of these conditions must have been variable then, as well as unquantifiable now: we may, however, imagine that sites probably thrived and were left from time to time, but later returned to. A recent demonstration of this has been the discovery of Viking occupation on the site of a Romano-British settlement at Gauber High Pasture in upper Ribblesdale.[22] A striking view of how long term this process might be is the recently excavated site immediately to the south of the fort at Maiden Castle on Stainmore, where the latest structure on a site that showed both pre-Roman and Roman activity is a nineteenth-century cottage.[23]

Thus, the last years of the occupation obviously show a decline in (eventually) the degree of Roman military commitment, and therefore the ability of the population to continue its established life-style. These same last years, however, do not show any desire on the part of the 'subject populations' to abandon, of their own will, what had become their way of life over nearly four centuries; even the 'independence' revolt of 408 was basically over the question of how best to preserve the accepted life-style. Thus sometimes in small ways and sometimes in more significant ones the Romanisation of North-West England survived well beyond the physical ability of the population actually to fight for it.

Notes

(N.B. References to modern books and articles are given in an abbreviated form; these references are itemised in full in the Bibliography.)

1. For Hadrian's Wall, see Breeze and Dobson (1976), 202f.
2. *RIB* 605.
3. Johnson (1980), 83ff; Wilkes (1965).
4. Gillam (1949).
5. Mann (1974).
6. Eusebius *Vit. Const.* I, 8 and 25.
7. Zosimus II, 34.
8. *RIB* 616 and *RIB* 617; these statuettes are now lost: Shotter (1973b).
9. *RIB* 601; Shotter (1973b).
10. Bellhouse (1955).
11. Simpson and Hodgson (1947).
12. Ammianus Marcellinus XIV, 5, 6–9; Hind (1983), 1ff.
13. as Ammianus calls it (XXVII, 8).
14. Salway (1981), 374f.
15. Ammianus XXVII 3, 8.
16. Potter (1979).
17. Bellhouse (1953) (Wreay Hall); Collingwood (1931) (Barrock Fell).
18. Johnson (1980), 98.
19. Johnson (1980), 103; Miller (1975).
20. e.g. Barker (1975).
21. Birley, R. (1977); Salway (1980).
22. King (1978).
23. Clare, T.: excavation report will appear in a forthcoming volume of *CW²*.

7
Conclusions

Whilst a tolerably clear picture has developed over the years of the effects of the Roman occupation of North-West England, there is clearly great scope for new enquiry.

The military aspect of the occupation—forts and roads—has received a good deal of attention; the location of permanent forts must be reasonably complete, although the discovery of some new ones should not be precluded. A far greater lacuna is the chronology of occupation of the forts; very few have as yet anything more than a very basic chronological framework, and in particular it may well be that a number of the known forts have smaller—perhaps Agricolan—predecessors awaiting discovery. The character of the forts and their garrison patterns requires more work—in particular, the military occupation of Carlisle and the question of whether or not it is of a legionary character. It is possible that, as more writing-tablets are recovered from the waterlogged deposits of north-west sites, these may reveal information concerning military dispositions. On the military side, the least well-known aspect is the very earliest occupation—or more properly, the pattern of conquest. The earthwork remains of marching-camps survive poorly in land subject to ploughing, and it is the locations of these that are most likely to show us how the Roman army approached the problem of conquering the Brigantes.

The installations of the coast also, although they have now yielded a basic framework—both topographical and chronological—of development and occupation, still leave room for the elucidation of details; this is especially true of its physical extent and the question of how far different parts of the coast may have been treated in different ways. A further question concerns such use as may have been made of the installations in the fourth century.

The *vici*, too, leave many unanswered questions; in particular we have no satisfactory explanation as to why a considerable number of them seem not to have outlasted the mid-third century. Were there local conditions which were responsible, or was a more general factor at play? As yet we do not have, except on aerial photographs, anything like the full plan of a *vicus* in the North West. This not only denies us a full picture of all the buildings that these small towns might support, but also a reasonable idea of the make-up of the population. The organisation of the *vici* also requires further research.

In the countryside, the need is for excavation to answer some of the basic problems about development, chronology and economy; besides this the question of the economic relationship between the farms and the Roman sites needs further exploration, particularly through studies of bones and seeds from the Roman sites themselves. It should also be remembered that considerable areas of the North West have as yet not been flown or are not conducive to that form of reconnaissance.

These are *a few* of the problems requiring attention: however, in outline we do have a fair picture of the political growth of the Roman North West. Studies of the immediately post-Roman period and of the so-called 'Dark Ages' may well help to illuminate the question of whether Roman influence went deep or whether it was a passing phase, though it has to be admitted that Christianity in the Celtic West must have done a good deal to preserve a Roman tradition.

In conclusion, however, we now know enough to lay aside the older notions of an iron-fisted conqueror controlling a people generally hostile or sullenly passive. Rather, *Dea Brigantia* presided over territory that was in its way as Romanised as many other parts of the Empire.

Appendix I
The Brigantes, Venutius and Cartimandua

The two fullest accounts of the Brigantes are those of Tacitus in *Histories* III, 45, and *Annals* XII, 40. The latter, although written later, describes the earlier of the two situations. Whilst there are shades of difference between the two accounts, both stress that at least some of the squabbling between Venutius and Cartimandua remained internal to the Brigantes, although the former was able to call on help from outside—presumably from North Wales. It is also tolerably clear that the overall effect of the tensions was actually to maintain the *status quo*. The fact that Tacitus compares Venutius and Caratacus as warriors is itself of interest, and would certainly help to explain how the Brigantes were so formidable with him (that is, during Cerialis' governorship), and so much easier when he had been removed (that is, when Agricola went through the area in a single season).

(1) *Annals* XII, 40 (Events in the A.D. 50s)

However, since Caratacus' capture the best strategist was Venutius, a Brigantian. While married to the tribal queen, Cartimandua, he had remained loyal and under Roman protection. But divorce had immediately been followed by hostilities against her and then against us. At first, the Brigantes had merely fought among themselves. Cartimandua had astutely trapped Venutius' brother and other relatives. But her enemies, infuriated and goaded by fears of humiliating feminine rule, invaded her kingdom with a powerful force of picked warriors. We had foreseen this, and sent auxiliary battalions to support her. The engagement that followed had no positive results at first but ended more favourably. A battle fought by a regular brigade likewise had a satisfactory ending. Didius of impressive seniority and incapacitated by age, was content to act through subordinates and on the defensive. These campaigns were conducted by two imperial governors over a period of years. But I have described them in one place since piecemeal description would cast a strain on the memory. Now I return to the chronological succession of events.

(Extract from Tacitus, *The Annals of Imperial Rome*, trans. Michael Grant (Penguin Classics, Revised edition 1977), p. 269. Copyright © Michael Grant Publications Ltd, 1956, 1959, 1971. Reprinted by permission of Penguin Books Ltd.)

(2) *Histories III, 45* (Events leading up to full Roman intervention in the A.D. 70s)

. . . the spate of rumours about civil war, emboldened the Britons to pluck up their courage and follow a man called Venutius, who, quite apart from a violent character and a hatred of all things Roman, was goaded to fury by a personal feud with Queen Cartimandua. She had been for some time ruler of the Brigantes, and was a princess of high birth and hence influence. This she had increased thanks to her treacherous capture of King Caratacus, an action by which she was generally thought to have set the seal upon Claudius' triumph. Hence came wealth and the self-indulgence of prosperity. She tired of Venutius, who was her consort, and gave her hand and kingdom to his armour-bearer, one Vellocatus. This scandal immediately shook the royal house to its foundations. The discarded husband could rely on the support of the Brigantian people, the lover upon the infatuation of the queen and her ruthless cruelty. So Venutius summoned help from outside, and a simultaneous revolt on the part of the Brigantes themselves reduced Cartimandua to a position of acute danger, in which she appealed for Roman assistance. In the event, our cohorts and cavalry regiments did succeed, at the cost of desperate fighting, in rescuing the queen from a tight corner. Venutius inherited the throne, and we the fighting.

(Extract from Tacitus, *The Histories*, trans. Kenneth Wellesley (Penguin Classics, Revised edition 1972), pp. 172–72. Copyright © Kenneth Wellesley 1964, 1972. Reprinted by permission of Penguin Books Ltd.)

Appendix II
Known Dispositions of Roman Units

Chester	Leg II Adiutrix Leg XX Valeria Victrix (inscriptions give dates from mid-second to mid-third century)
Manchester	Vex of Leg II and III Italica (late second century) Coh I Frisiavonum Coh III Bracaraugustanorum (possibly second century)
Castleshaw	Coh III Bracaraugustanorum
Ribchester	Ala II Astrurum Numerus Equitum (later Ala) Sarmatarum (third century)
Lancaster	Ala Augusta Ala Sebosiana (mid-third century) Numerus Barcariorum
Slack	Coh IIII Breucorum
Bainbridge	Coh VI Nerviorum (early-third century)
Bowes	Coh IIII Breucorum (130s) Coh I Thracum (late second to mid-third century)
Kirkby Thore	Ala Numerus militum Syrorum Sagittariorum
Brougham	Coh ? Gallorum Coh I Vangionum (?) Cuneus Frisionum Germanorum Numerus Equitum Stratonicianorum
Hardknott	Coh IIII Delmatorum (Hadrianic)
Moresby	Coh II Thracum Coh II Lingonum
Maryport	Coh I Hispanorum Equitata (Hadrianic) Coh I Delmatarum (Antonine) Coh I Baetasiorum
Beckfoot	Coh II Pannoniorum
Papcastle	Cuneus Frisionum Aballavensium (mid-third century)
Old Carlisle	Ala Augusta (late second to mid-third century)
Old Penrith	Coh II Gallorum Equitata (mid-third century) Vex Marsacarum (mid-third century) Vex Germanorum (mid-third century)
Carlisle	Ala Augusta Petriana milliaria torquata (late second century)
Netherby	Coh I Nervana Coh I Aelia Hispanorum milliaria equitata (early to mid-third century)
Bewcastle	Coh I Dacorum
Vindolanda	Coh II Nerviorum (?) Coh III Nerviorum Coh IIII Gallorum (third century)

Great Chesters	Vex Raetorum Gaesatorum
	Coh Raetorum (mid-second century)
	Coh VI Nerviorum
	Coh II Asturum (early to mid-third century)
Carvoran	Coh I Hamiorum Sagittariorum (Hadrianic, late Antonine)
	Coh II Delmatarum
	Coh I Batavorum
	Numerus
Birdoswald	Coh I Aelia Dacorum (third century)
	Coh I Thracum C.R. (early third century)
	Coh ? (late third century)
Castlesteads	Coh IIII Gallorum Equitata
	Coh II Tungrorum milliaria equitata C.L. (mid-third century)
	Equites
Burgh-by-Sands	Coh I Nervana Germanorum milliaria equitata
	Numerus Maurorum Aurelianorum (mid-third century)
Bowness-on-Solway	Coh ? (mid-third century)
Birrens	Coh II Tungrorum milliaria equitata C.L. (Antonine)
	Coh I Nervana Germanorum milliaria equitata
Melandra Castle	Coh I Frisiavonum
Brough-on-Noe	Coh I Aquitanorum
Whitley Castle	Coh II Nerviorum

Appendix III

Dated Building-work at North-West Forts

A.	*Vespasian*	Chester (A.D. 79)	*RIB* 463 and *EE* IX, 1039
			Britannia I (1970), 292f.
B.	*Trajan*	Chester (A.D. 102–117)	*RIB* 464
		Lancaster (A.D. 102–117)	*RIB* 604
		Melandra (A.D. 98–117)	*RIB* 208
C.	*Hadrian*	Bowes (A.D. 130–3)	*RIB* 739
		Hardknott	*JRS* 55 (1965), 222
		Moresby (A.D. 128–138)	*RIB* 801
		Maryport (A.D. 117–138)	*RIB* 851
		Netherby	*RIB* 974
		Bewcastle	*RIB* 995
		Vindolanda (?)	*RIB* 1702
		Great Chesters (A.D. 128–138)	*RIB* 1736
		Carvoran (A.D. 128–138)	*RIB* 1808, 1820 (136–138)
D.	*Antoninus Pius*	Castlesteads (A.D. 140–4)	*RIB* 1997
		Birrens (A.D. 157–8)	*RIB* 2110
		Brough-on-Noe (A.D. 158)	*RIB* 283
E.	*Marcus Aurelius*	Ribchester (A.D. 163–6)	*RIB* 589
		Hardknott (A.D. 163–6)	*RIB* 793
		Vindolanda (A.D. 163–6)	*RIB* 1703
		Great Chesters (A.D. 166–9)	*RIB* 1737
		Carvoran (A.D. 163–6)	*RIB* 1809
F.	*Septimius Severus*	Chester (A.D. 194–6)	*RIB* 465
		Manchester	*RIB* 581
		Bainbridge (A.D. 205–8)	*RIB* 722, 723
		Greta Bridge (A.D. 205–8)	*RIB* 746
		Bowes (A.D. 205–8)	*RIB* 740
		Brough (A.D. 197)	*RIB* 757
		Birdoswald (A.D. 198–209)	*RIB* 1910
G.	*Caracalla*	Maryport (A.D. 211–17)	*RIB* 832, 850
		Old Carlisle (A.D. 213)	*RIB* 928
		Netherby (A.D. 213)	*RIB* 976, 977
		Vindolanda (A.D. 213)	*RIB* 1705
		Birdoswald (A.D. 211–17)	*RIB* 1911
		Whitley Castle (A.D. 213 and 215–16)	*RIB* 1202, 1203
H.	*Elagabalus*	Birdoswald (A.D. 219)	*RIB* 1914
I.	*Severus Alexander*	Ribchester (A.D. 222–235)	*RIB* 587
		Old Penrith (A.D. 222–235)	*RIB* 919, 929
		Old Carlisle (A.D. 222–235)	*RIB* 929
		Netherby (A.D. 222)	*RIB* 978
		Vindolanda (A.D. 223)	*RIB* 1706
		Great Chesters (A.D. 225)	*RIB* 1738
J.	*Gordian III*	Maryport (A.D. 238–244)	*RIB* 854
		Stanwix (A.D. 238–244)	*RIB* 2027
K.	*Postumus*	Lancaster (A.D. 262–6)	*RIB* 605
L.	*Diocletian*	Birdoswald (A.D. 297–305)	*RIB* 1912

Notes and Abbreviations

Note: The majority of the military sites discussed in this book have seen excavation over a long period of time, which has meant that all but a few items from the detailed references for individual sites has had, for reasons of space, to be omitted. However, extremely useful summaries and bibliographies for the military sites may be found in M. J. Jones, *Roman Fort-Defences to* A.D. 117, British Archaeological Reports No. 21 (Oxford 1975). In addition, the annual surveys entitled 'Roman Britain in 19 . . .', contained first in *Journal of Roman Studies* and (since 1970) in *Britannia* provide on-going and up-to-the-minute summaries of current excavations. At the time of writing, several major excavation Reports and Site Studies are awaited or actually in the press—Carlisle, Blackfriars Street (M. R. McCarthy), Lancaster (G. D. B. Jones and D. C. A. Shotter), Ribchester (B. J. N. Edwards and P. V. Webster), Wilderspool (J. Hinchcliffe and J. H. Williams), and most recently Walton-le-Dale and Papcastle (A. C. H. Olivier).

Abbreviations

JRS	Journal of Roman Studies
RIB	R. G. Collingwood and R. P Wright, *Roman Inscriptions of Britain* (Oxford 1965), Vol. 1: Inscriptions on Stone
CW²	Transactions of the Cumberland and Westmorland Antiquarian and Archaeological Society, Series 2
Arch. Journ.	Archaeological Journal
Arch. Ael.	Archaeologia Aeliana
SHA	Scriptores Historiae Augustae
PSAS	Proceedings of the Society of Antiquaries of Scotland
EE	Ephemeris Epigraphica
CAJ	Journal of the Chester Archaeological Society
YAJ	Yorkshire Archaeological Journal
RCHM	Royal Commission on Historical Monuments, England: Westmorland (London 1936)

Bibliography

Barker, P. (1975). Excavations at the Baths Basilica at Wroxeter 1966–74. *Britannia* VI, 106–17.

Bellhouse, R. L. (1953). A Roman Fort at Wreay Hall, near Carlisle. *CW²* 53, 49–51.

Bellhouse, R. L. (1954a). A newly-discovered Roman Fort at Park House, near Carlisle. *CW²* 54, 9–16.

Bellhouse, R. L. (1954b). Roman Sites on the Cumberland Coast 1954. *CW²*, 28–55.

Bellhouse, R. L. (1955). The Roman Fort at Burrow Walls, near Workington. *CW²* 55, 30–45.

Bellhouse, R. L. (1960a). The Roman Forts near Caermote. *CW²* 60, 20–3.

Bellhouse, R. L. (1960b). Excavations in Eskdale, the Muncaster Roman Kilns. *CW²* 60, 1–12.

Bellhouse, R. L. (1967). The Aughertree Fell Enclosures. *CW²* 67, 26–30.

Bellhouse, R. L. (1981). Hadrian's Wall: The Limiting Ditches in the Cardurnock Peninsular. *Britannia* XII, 135–42.

Bellhouse, R. L. and Richardson, G. G. S. (1982). The Trajanic Fort at Kirkbride; the terminus of the Stanegate Frontier. *CW²* 82, 35–50.

Birley, A. R. (1973). Petillius Cerialis and the Conquest of Brigantia. *Britannia* IV, 179–90.

Birley, A. R. (1975). Agricola, the Flavian Dynasty and Tacitus, in Levick, B. (Ed.) *The Ancient Historian and his Materials*, pp.139–54 (Farnborough, Hants).

Birley, E. B. (1932). Materials for the History of Roman Brougham. *CW²* 32, 124–39.

Birley, E. B. (1946). The Roman Site at Burrow-in-Lonsdale. *CW²* 46, 126–56.

Birley, E. B. (1947). The Roman Fort at Low Borrow Bridge. *CW²* 47, 1–19.

Birley, E. B. (1951). The Roman Fort and Settlement at Old Carlisle. *CW²* 51, 16–39.

Birley, E. B. (1953). The Roman Milestone at Middleton-in-Lonsdale. *CW²* 53, 52–62.

Birley, E. B. (1958). The Roman Fort at Brough-under-Stainmore. *CW²* 58, 31–56.

Birley, E. B. (1963). Roman Papcastle. *CW²* 63, 96–125.

Birley, R. N. (1977). Vindolanda; A Roman Frontier Post on Hadrian's Wall. (London).

Blake, B. (1959). Excavations of Native (Iron Age) Sites in Cumberland 1956–58. *CW²* 59, 1–14.

Bowman, A. K. and Thomas, J. D. (1983). *Vindolanda: The Latin Writing Tablets*. Britannia Monographs 4. (London).

Branigan, K. (1980). Villas in the North: Change in the Rural Landscape, in Branigan, K. (Ed.) *Rome and the Brigantes*, pp.18–27 (Sheffield)

Breeze, D. J. (1975). The Abandonment of the Antonine Wall: its date and implications. *Scot. Arch. Forum* 7, 67–78.

Breeze, D. J. and Dobson, B. (1976). *Hadrian's Wall*. (London).

Bruton, F. A. (1908). *Excavation of the Roman Forts at Castleshaw*. (Manchester).

Bruton, F. A. (1909). *The Roman Fort at Manchester*. (Manchester).

Collingwood, R. G. (1931). A Roman Fortlet on Barrock Fell, near Low Hesket. *CW²* 31, 111–18.

Collingwood, W. G. (1908–9). Report on an Exploration of the Romano–British Settlement at Ewe Close. *CW²* 9, 295–309.

Charlesworth, D. (1964). Recent Work at Kirkby Thore. *CW²* 64, 61–75.

Charlesworth, D. (1965). Excavations at Papcastle 1961–62. *CW²* 65, 102–14.

Davies, R. W. (1977). Cohors I Hispanorum and the Garrisons of Maryport. *CW²* 77, 7–16.

Davies, R. W. (1971). The Roman Military Diet. *Britannia* II, 122–42.

Edwards, B. J. N. (1972). *Ribchester*. National Trust Handbook.

Gillam, J. P. (1949). Also, Along the Line of the Wall. *CW²* 49, 38–58.

Goodburn, R. and Bartholomew, P. (eds.), (1976). *Aspects of the Notitia Dignitatum*. British Archaeological Reports 15. (Oxford).

Hassall, M. W. C. (1976). Britain in the *Notitia*. In Goodburn R. and Bartholomew P. (Eds.): *vide supra*, pp. 103–117.

Hartley, B. R. (1966). Some Problems of the Roman Military Occupation of Northern England. *Northern History I*, 7–10.

Hartley, B. R. (1972). The Roman Occupations of Scotland: the Evidence of Samian Ware. *Britannia* III, 1–55.

Hartley, B. R. (1980). The Brigantes and the Roman Army, in Branigan K. (Ed.) *Rome and the Brigantes*, pp. 2–7 (Sheffield).

Hanson, W. S., with Daniels, C. M., Dore J. N., and Gilliam, J. P (1979). The Agricolan Supply-base at Red House, Corbridge. *Arch Ael.⁵* VII, 1–88.

Heurgon, J. (1951). The Amiens Patera. *JRS* 41, 22–4.

Higham, N. J. (1978). Early Field Survival in North Cumbria, in Bowen, H. C. and Fowler, P. J. (Eds.) *Early Land Allotment in the British Isles*. British Archaeological Reports 48, pp. 119–25 (Oxford).

Higham, N. J. (1979). An Aerial Survey of the Upper Lune Valley. In Higham N. J. (Ed.) *The Changing Past*, pp. 31–8. (Manchester).

Higham, N. J. (1980). Native Settlements West of the Pennines. In Branigan, K. (Ed.) *Rome and the Brigantes*, pp. 41–7. (Sheffield).

Higham, N. J. (1982). 'Native' Settlements on the North Slopes of the Lake District. *CW²* 82, 29–33.

Higham, N. J. and Jones G. D. B. (1975). Frontier, Forts and Farmers. *Arch Journ.* 132, 16–53.

Hildyard, E. J. W. (1951). Renewed Excavation at Low Borrow Bridge. *CW²* 51, 40–66.

Hildyard, E. J. W. (1954). Excavations at Burrow-in-Lonsdale. *CW²* 54, 66–101.

Hill, P. V. (1970). *The Undated Coins of Rome*, A.D. 98–148. (London).

Hind, J. G. F. (1977). The 'Genounian' Part of Britain. *Britannia* VIII, 229–34.

Hind, J. G. F. (1983). Who betrayed Britain to the Barbarians in A.D. 367? *Northern History* 19, 1–7.

Hogg, R. (1965). Excavation of the Roman auxiliary tilery, Brampton. *CW²* 65, 133–68.

Jarrett, M. G. (1976). *Maryport, Cumbria: A Roman Fort and its Garrison.* (Kendal).

Johnson, A. S. (1980). *Later Roman Britain.* (London).

Jones, G. D. B. (1968). The Romans in the North West. *Northern History* III, 1–26.

Jones, G. D. B. (1970). Roman Lancashire. *Arch. Journ.* 127, 237–45.

Jones, G. D. B. (1972). Excavations at Northwich (Condate). *Arch. Journ.* 128, 31–77.

Jones, G. D. B. (1974). *Roman Manchester.* (Altrincham).

Jones, G. D. B. (1975). The North-Western Interface, in Fowler, P. J. (Ed.) *Recent work in Rural Archaeology*, pp. 93–106 (Bradford-on-Avon).

Jones, G. D. B. (1979). The Future of Aerial Photography in the North. In Higham, N. J. (Ed.) *The Changing Past*, pp. 75–87. (Manchester).

Jones, G. D. B. (1980). Archaeology and Coastal Change in the North-West, in Thompson, F. H. (Ed.) *Archaeology and Coastal Change*, pp. 87–102 (London).

Jones, G. D. B. (1982). The Solway Frontier: Interim Report 1976–81. *Britannia* XIII, 284–97.

Jones, G. D. B. and Wild, J. P. (1970). Manchester University Excavations at Brough-on-Noe (Navio) 1969. *Derbys. Arch. Journ.* 70, 99–106.

Jones, M. J. (1975). *Roman Fort-Defences to A.D. 117.* British Archaeological Reports 21. (Oxford).

Jones, M. J. (1977). Archaeological Work at Brough-under-Stainmore 1971–72, I. The Roman Discoveries. *CW²* 77, 35–50.

Jones, R. F. J. (1981). Change in the Frontier, Northern Britain in the Third Century, in King A. and Henig, M. *The Roman West in the Third Century*, BAR(S) 109, pp. 393–414.

Keppie, L. J. F. and Walker, J. J. (1981). Fortlets on the Antonine Wall at Seabegs Wood, Kinneil and Cleddans. *Britannia* XII, 143–62.

King, A. (1978). Gauber High Pasture, Ribblehead—an interim report, in Hall, R. A. (Ed.) *Viking Age York and the North*, CBA Research Report 27, pp. 21–25 (London).

Lowndes, R. A. C. (1963). 'Celtic' fields, farms and burial mounds in the Lune Valley. *CW²* 63, 77–95.

Lowndes, R. A. C. (1964). Excavation of a Romano-British Farmstead at Eller Beck. *CW²* 64, 1–13.

Mann, J. C. (1974). The Northern Frontier after A.D. 369. *Glasgow Arch. Journ.* 3, 34–42.

Manning, W. H. (1975). Economic influences on land use in the military areas of the Highland Zone during the Roman period. In Evans, J. G., Limbrey, S. and Cleere, H. (Eds.) *The Effect of Man on the Landscape: the Highland Zone.* CBA Research Report 11, pp. 112–16. (London).

McCarthy, M. R. (1980). *Carlisle, a Frontier City.* (Carlisle).

Miller, M. (1975). Stilicho's Pictish War. *Britannia* VI, 141–45.

Pennington, W. (1970). Vegetation History in the North-West of England: a regional synthesis, in Walker D. and West, R. G. (Eds.) *Studies in the Vegetational History of the British Isles*, pp. 41–79 (Cambridge).

Potter, T. W. J. (1977). The Biglands Milefortlet and the Cumberland Coast Defences. *Britannia* VIII, 149–83.

Potter, T. W. J. (1979). *The Romans in North-West England.* (Kendal).

Poulter, A. (1982). Old Penrith: Excavations 1977 and 1979. *CW²* 82, 51–66.

Richardson, A. (1982). Evidence for Centuriation in the Inglewood Forest. *CW²* 82, 67–71.

Richardson, G. G. S. (1977). A Romano-British Farmstead at Fingland. *CW²* 77, 53–9.

Richardson, G. G. S. and Richardson, A. (1980). A Possible Roman Road in the Kirkstone Pass and Matterdale. *CW²* 80, 160–2.

Richmond, I. A. (1933). Castlefolds by Great Asby. *CW²* 33, 233–7.

Richmond, I. A. (1935). The Rudge Cup: II. The Inscription. *Arch. Ael⁴* 12, 334–42.

Richmond, I. A. (1936). Roman Leaden-Sealings from Brough-under-Stainmore. *CW²* 36, 104–25.

Richmond, I. A. (1945). The Sarmatae, Bremetennacum Veteranorum and the Regio Bremetennacensis. *JRS* 35, 15–29.

Richmond, I. A. (1951). A Roman Arterial Signalling System in the Stainmore Pass, in Grimes, W. F. (Ed.) *Aspects of Archaeology in Britain Beyond*, pp. 293-302 (London).

Richmond, I. A. (1954). Queen Cartimandua. *JRS* 44, 43-52.

Richmond, I. A. and Crawford, O. G. S. (1949). The British Section of the *Ravenna Cosmography*. *Archaeologia* 93, 1–50.

Richmond, I. A. and McIntyre, J. (1934). The Roman Camps at Rey Cross and Crackenthorpe. *CW²* 34, 50–61.

Rivet, A. L. F. (1970). The British Section of the *Antonine Itinerary*. *Britannia* I, 34–82.

Robertson, A. S. (1973). *The Antonine Wall*. (Glasgow).

St. Joseph, J. K. S. (1951). Air Reconnaissance of North Britain. *JRS* 41, 52-65.

Salway, P. (1980). The *Vici*: Urbanisation in the North, in Branigan, K. (Ed.) *Rome and the Brigantes*, pp. 8–17 (Sheffield).

Salway, P. (1981). *Roman Britain*. (Oxford).

Shotter, D. C. A. (1973a). *Romans in Lancashire*. (Clapham, Yorks).

Shotter, D. C. A. (1973b). *Numeri Barcariorum*: A Note on *RIB* 601. *Britannia* IV, 206–9.

Shotter, D. C. A. (1976). Coin Evidence and the Northern Frontier in the Second Century A.D. *PSAS* 107, 81–91.

Shotter, D. C. A. (1978a). Roman Coins From Carlisle. *CW²* 78, 201–3.

Shotter, D. C. A. (1978b). Three Early Imperial Hoards from Lancashire. *Coin Hoards* 4, 44–5.

Shotter, D. C. A. (1979). The Evidence of Coin-Loss and the Roman Occupation of North-West England, in Higham, N. J. (Ed.) *The Changing Past*, pp. 1–13 (Manchester).

Shotter, D. C. A. (1980). Roman Coins from Starling Castle. *CW²* 80, 163.

Shotter, D. C. A. (1983). A Note on Tiles found on the Mitre Yard, Lancaster in 1973. *Britannia* XIV, 270–1.

Simpson, F. G. and Hodgson, K. S. (1947). The Coastal Milefortlet at Cardurnock. *CW²* 47, 78–127.

Thompson, F. H. (1965). *Roman Cheshire*. (Chester).

Thompson, F. H. (1976). The Excavation of the Roman Amphitheatre of Chester. *Archaeologia* 105, 127–239.

Thompson, F. H. (Ed.) (1980). *Archaeology and Coastal Change*. (London).

Tylecote, R. F. (1962). *Metallurgy in Archaeology*. (London).

Ward, J. H. (1973). The British Sections of the *Notitia Dignitatum*: an alternative interpretation. *Britannia* IV, 253–63.

Webster, G. (1970). *The Roman Imperial Army*. (London).

Webster, P. V. (1975). The Later Roman Occupation at Wilderspool. *CAJ* 58, 91–2.

Wilkes, J. J. (1965). Early Fourth-Century Rebuilding in Hadrian's Wall Forts, in Jarrett, M. G. and Dobson, B. (Eds.) *Britain and Rome*, pp. 114–38 (Kendal).